TWO TOGETHER

ROBERT C. DODDS

Two Together

A Handbook for Your Marriage

THOMAS Y. CROWELL COMPANY

NEW YORK · ESTABLISHED 1834

"Can two walk together, except they be agreed?"

AMOS 3:3

TO ELISABETH,

MARGARET, ANDREW AND PAUL,

welcome participants
in the marriage I know best

Contents

xii · *Contents*

TWO TOGETHER

CHAPTER ONE:

A matter of wonder

ONE OF my professional duties has been to stand in the front of a church and watch as two trembling young people come forward to take each other in Christian marriage. They have a right to be awestruck at what they are doing. They are embarking upon a venture where the stakes are high in joy or agony. Sometimes they appear to me, as I watch them, to have been well prepared for marriage by years of secure family relationships. Sometimes, however, their personalities are irritable, moody, or insecure.

When they begin to exchange the momentous words of their marriage vows, I am the only person in the church seeing the expressions on their faces and I feel an overwhelming responsibility for the authority that has been given me "to join together this man and this woman in holy matrimony."

And I am filled with wonder, too. The words and symbols of this service are simple and beautiful and terribly profound. The man takes the woman's hand and looks at her. "I take thee," he begins to say. I glance up, and the other faces in the congregation reflect the wonder which I feel. A few are touched with tears—of joy or of apprehension? A few are beaming brightly with incandescent happiness. All are listening earnestly. Everyone seems to sense that this is the climactic moment when, by the grace of God, a marriage is being created.

The wonders of marriage are many. That two distinct individuals should wish to live together for a lifetime is one thing; that they should pledge themselves to each other with such dramatic intensity is another. But the greatest wonder of all is that so many marriages should be blessed with harmony. In spite of great pressures and obstacles, many marriages develop into real families.

The future of the family, and of marriage itself, depends upon the man and the woman who stand in front of a minister to exchange their vows. A short generation ago the family was being lamented as a disappearing institution. But today the American family seems to be coming back upon the scene with renewed vigor and stability. Part of the reason lies in the firm intention of the couples who are marrying. Another part lies in their insistent request for adequate premarital preparation. Perhaps another part of the reason is that young people in our world have been made wise by living in an age of terrible strain.

ARE YOU READY?

You have now begun to talk with each other about your marriage. A new note of wonder has entered your lives as you have begun to dream and to discuss your future life together. You can look ahead and imagine clearly the wedding date, the church and minister, and you yourselves taking part in the drama of the service. You can look beyond that day to the experiences you will share. You are filled with a sense of mystery as you try to understand the love which is tying you closer and closer to one another.

And at the same time you are filled with many questions. Practical questions about the wedding itself—the procedure for getting a license, the proper clothes to wear, the invitations, the friends who will stand beside you, the purchase of the rings and the place of the reception. Your minister will be able to give you practical, step-by-step advice on many of the matters which you need to settle soon. He can be your guide on what is good usage and help you plan the arrangements. He will want to prepare you for marriage. It is a good practice to consult your minister as soon as your marriage seems certain.

But there are other questions, too, which you may be asking. Are you actually ready to marry? Are you really in love with each other? How can you be sure? Are you properly matched? What will marriage be like? No one can give you firm and positive answers to questions like these. Will yours be a happy marriage? No one can say for sure.

The questions, of course, are important, and it is better to raise them now than later. Their solution is urgent to your happiness. As you seek your own answers, four approaches may be helpful to you.

In the first place, remember that such questions are very natural. Most couples wonder about them often. Matrimony, as the marriage service says, "is not by any to be entered into unadvisedly or lightly." The great ventures of life cannot be dealt with casually. It is quite likely that you will be nervous and full of questions as you approach your wedding day. You can, though, reduce the element of risk. You can make sensible preparations for a long life together. But at the last you have to step forth in trust. All the crucial choices of your life have to be made that way.

In the second place, you may wish to test your love against the opinions of your family and your friends. These people have had a chance to watch you from the outside, to decide whether you are matched to each other, and whether you are mature enough for marriage. You may want to take their opinions with a grain of salt. You may not want to hear their opinions at all. But many couples do find help in talking with their close associates.

THE PURPOSE OF THIS BOOK

In the third place, look as deeply as you can into what marriage really is. This book has been designed as an attempt to introduce you to the inward meanings of matrimony. It has been prepared, not for the experts, but for you, the least experienced beginners; not to give you well-rounded answers, but to set you in search of your own answers. It has been designed for you, as you contemplate the wonderful and beckoning mysteries of marriage. You owe it to yourselves to try to understand in advance what your marriage is likely to be.

In the fourth place, talk with each other. This suggestion may sound absurd at first, because for months now you have been looking ahead and talking about every kind of possibility. From what you like to eat to how you will raise your children or what kind of house you will buy, you have already found points of difference. From what you seek in amusement to whom you choose for friends, you may already have uncovered strains. Where will you live? What will you do together? How many children will you have? Are marriages made in heaven, and have you only one soul mate in the whole world?

You have found many things to laugh over, to talk about, to disagree over. Your talk on these matters has been an essential part of your preparation for marriage. And you have found that it can be fun as well.

The purpose of this book, however, is to give you a few more ideas for things to talk about together. Already you have no shortage of conversational subjects. But, some of these suggestions may not have occurred to you before; some of them will seem to reveal old topics in a new light. All of them can have a direct bearing on the future harmony of your marriage. The main thing is that you should begin to discuss them frankly with each other *before you marry*. Many couples before you have done so with profit.

JOY IN MARRIAGE

In one sense you are already having a preview of your marriage. The period of your courtship and your engagement ought to give you a fair taste of what is to come. If your engagement has been very long, or if your relationship has been very intense you may have experienced some extra problems. These may disappear when you marry. But you should already have been learning some of the secrets of married harmony. Or, if you have not, you might be wise to postpone your wedding date and take more time for courting.

A key to your relationship is the joy you find in being together. It is the spontaneous affection you feel toward each other, the experiences you want to share, and the laughter you enjoy. This joy shows up in the way you exchange glances across the dance floor, in the way your thoughts are always finding room for each other even when you are miles apart. This joy sustains you through your disagreements and through the strains in your relationship. You keep coming back to the central fact of your courtship and find that it is joy.

And if the note of joy is missing, or if joy has been

lost through the problems of your courtship, then you have reason to wonder whether you should marry. You are not likely to change very much just because a minister has declared you husband and wife, nor will the reading of the marriage service do much to alter the way you treat each other. A joyless life together does not contain much promise.

Years of married life, of course, may change the quality of your joy. By the grace of God, it can become deeper and more mature. You may not act like newlyweds forever, but you can have abiding joy in your relationship.

In marriage two lives are uniquely joined together. Two people share each other's past and a common future. They share house, money, and family. They share physically in the sex relationship. They raise children and take vacations together. They are joined to each other in happiness and sorrows, in success and failure. They belong to each other in the laughing exuberance of their youth and in the reveries of their old age.

The variety and the wonder of marriage is inexhaustible. You have already begun to discover some of its wonder for yourselves.

SOME BOOKS SUGGESTING THE
WONDER OF MARRIAGE

DEROUGEMONT, DENIS. *Love in the Western World*. Pantheon Books, Inc., New York.
A careful, rather scholarly survey of love as it appears in Western history, literature, ideas, myths and practices. Well written. The last section is especially interesting in terms of marriage.

DELAND, MARGARET CAMPBELL. *Golden Yesterdays*. Harper & Brothers, New York.
The autobiography of a woman who had an outstandingly happy marriage. A heartwarming counter-balance to the gloomy pictures sometimes described.

BOWEN, ELIZABETH. *A World of Love*. Alfred A. Knopf, Inc., New York.
A novel by a skillful English writer about a woman who did not marry her "great love," but settled for a second choice. After years of dreariness, this couple finally discovers each other. Each of them, they realize, is a person in need of tenderness, and this discovery salvages their marriage.

WEST, JESSAMYN. *The Friendly Persuasion*. Harcourt, Brace and Company, New York.
Fiction in a similar vein; warm, loving, humorous.

WEST, REBECCA. *The Thinking Reed*. Viking Press, New York.

A novel about the slow development of a close relationship between two people who marry without love, and gradually discover it.

JOYCE, JAMES. *The Dubliners*. Modern Library, New York. The closing short story in this book, "The Dead," reveals marvellously the thoughts of a man, pondering in middle age the meaning of a marriage which has been growing more wonderful with the ripening of the years. Good for reading aloud on wedding anniversaries.

CHAPTER TWO:

Humor and compromise

A NEWSPAPER once reported a wedding in the following succinct and ominous paragraph:

"Bob and Madeline were married on October 20, thus terminating a friendship that first began way back in junior high school."

The fact is that many a marriage has indeed terminated a beautiful friendship. The inescapable intimacies of marriage can introduce intolerable strains into the relationship between a man and a woman. Especially where two people are rigidly inflexible or somberly determined to have their own way, friendship can be weakened or destroyed.

On the other hand, of course, marriage can bring new depth and meaning to a friendship. Fortunately this happens often enough that you probably know a number of families in which the husband and wife enjoy a ripening and good-humored friendship, and you have reason for hoping that your experience will be like theirs. Naturally you wonder what factors can make the difference in your marriage.

High on the list you will want to place humor and the ability to compromise. The purpose of this chapter is to suggest how laughter and the arts of compromise contribute to a good marriage. Then we look at several aspects of marriage in which these twin qualities are especially important.

THE CAPACITY
FOR LAUGHTER

The gift of humor is born in a sense of the ironic so that one chuckles at what is inappropriate. It sees through what is pompous and enjoys the pinprick which releases air from the balloons of dignity. Humor brings gaiety to life and the virtues of self-insight and self-criticism. It brings a touch of light gentleness into a world which could be oppressively heavy. The serious business of humor is this: it sets life in perspective and makes people not only bearable but also endlessly interesting. The real essence of a sense of humor is that you are able to laugh at yourself.

There is a world of difference, of course, between ordinary, raucous laughter and a sense of humor. You may roar and be doubled over with laughter and still be a long way from that humor which transforms an ordinary marriage into a relationship of special joy.

You may be able to create an atmosphere of inflated pomposity around yourself at work. You may be able to carry this aura of majesty into your church and even into your social contacts. But in the intimacies of marriage, your pretensions are almost sure to collapse. Somewhere your fundamental humanity is sure to show. Like everyone else you will have to get into your trousers one leg at a time. Or you will snore. Or you will talk in your sleep.

One marriage of which I know got off to a fine start when the bride zealously starched her husband's underwear. The obvious ridiculousness of that situation got them laughing together at themselves. Children have their ways of putting pins in a person's self-esteem.

They contribute their own humorous achievements. They help a family to develop the special vocabulary of humor which is always its own.

No one likes to be laughed at unmercifully. No one enjoys being teased by someone who always has to maintain his own superiority. But everyone loves a sociable laugh. Laughter of that kind is a great leveller and has a way of reducing the person who needs it to his proper size. Some of the most delicious moments of your marriage will come as you learn together how to laugh at yourselves.

THE ART OF COMPROMISE

Closely related to a lively sense of humor is an ability in the arts of compromise, a skill which is crucially significant in the many adjustments of marriage. If you take yourself too seriously, if the delicate self-appraisals prompted by ridiculousness have never penetrated your spirit, if you always have to have your own way because you believe that you are always right, then serious consequences will ensue for your marriage. You will have to learn to make adjustments, or your marriage will have to build around your inflexibility, or your marriage will fall apart.

*How wide will the window be opened when you
go to sleep?*
Who will get up to feed the baby?
*How late at night will you stay up and how early
will you wake?*
*Will you take your vacation in the mountains or
at the shore?*
*Will you make an effort to see your old friends—
or your spouse's?*
Whose turn is it to get new clothes?
*How will you choose your house, your car, the
movies you see?*
How will you train your children?
Whose favorite TV program will you turn on?

I have known families in which the daily menu was
a matter for frequent adjustment. How often, for example, could turnips be served? The wife believed that
they contained necessary nutrients, and the husband
disdained them.

Jack Spratt and his wife, in the nursery rhyme, had
an ideal arrangement. One liked lean meat and the
other liked fat, so between them they licked the platter
clean. But the poem does not go on to describe the
ways Mr. and Mrs. Spratt had to adjust to each other and
compromise with each other. Every marriage has large

areas in which you bargain with each other, or arrange a temporary truce, or frankly bow to the will of the other. One of you cannot make all the concessions without weakening the fabric of your marriage. Nor can you live for long in separate armed camps. Your marriage will prosper as you explore, with good humor, the gentle arts of negotiation and compromise.

MALE AND FEMALE

The fundamental differences between the sexes will provide your marriage with an arena for the exercise of humor and compromise. Your differentness from each other has probably been as strong an appeal in your courtship as your similarities. Marriage will not blur you indistinguishably into each other. As long as you live, one of you will remain male and the other female, and the sheer fact of sex will affect each of your approaches to life. The miracle of marriage is that two people with such dramatic differences in their backgrounds, their experiences, their personalities and even in their bodies, can be united harmoniously over a period of many years. This miracle needs a man and a woman who try to understand and encourage the special contributions of the opposite sex.

A popular woman's magazine, for example, has run

a series of ads which stress the uniqueness of woman-
kind. A man may never really understand his wife,
these ads suggest, but he can love her unexpected,
mysterious, puzzling ways. He can enjoy her sudden
intuitions, her unreasonable reasonings, her tantalizing
forms of influence, her flashes of poetic truth. He can
encourage her to remain a person full of surprise and
paradox and wonder, but he cannot analyze her as he
might try to do with another man. She will always
baffle and amaze him. And I suppose that such ads as
these are calculated to persuade women to buy a magazine which emphasizes that they are not like men. If
they are successful in that purpose, then there must
be many women who want to stay apart from the inner
world of men, mysteriously perplexing and yet infinitely desirable.

Popular legend draws a clear line between masculinity
and femininity.

Masculine traits are supposed to be:	*Feminine traits are the opposite:*
Aggressiveness	Weakness
Boldness	Desire to be submissive
Frankness	Tenderness
Rationality	A tendency towards guile

Masculine traits are supposed to be:	*Feminine traits are the opposite:*
Objectivity	Greater need for security than for adventure
A tendency toward ruthlessness	Subjectivity
A desire to be dominant	The insights that come from poetry and intuition

The psychiatrists are now saying, however, that each person possesses both masculine and feminine traits. A man, for example, may have a capacity for gentleness and the tenderest kind of love, while a woman may be aggressive and quite dominant. Perhaps we cannot do much to alter the combination of characteristics which make up our personalities, but we can channel our efforts so as to develop some qualities while letting others lie dormant.

Or there is another angle from which to observe the difference between the sexes. Some authorities claim that the essential role of a woman is to have children and the essential purpose of a man is to work. The woman, by this view, needs to be a mother, to have babies and to raise children. All of her interests, her deepest needs and her potential contributions to marriage are moulded by this basic child-bearing drive. Even in courtship, these authorities say, a woman's plans are firmly fixed on the children she wants to have. A man, on the other hand, knows in a vague way that children often result from marriage, but the possibility of his becoming a father occurs to him only as a dim and distant fact. His basic and immediate interest is in his work and in all the implications of his job.

The trick of marriage seems to lie in the following directions:

1. Try to understand the mysterious traits of the opposite sex.

2. Accept the fact that the goals and approaches of a man and a woman are likely to be different.

3. Encourage and develop in each other the particular contributions that the other sex can bring.

4. With humor and grace, thank God for the differences that do exist.

The simple truth is that a man and a woman need each other.

Because of that need, love can grow between them.

Men marry what they need. I marry you,
morning by morning, day by day, night by night,
and every marriage makes this marriage new.

I marry you from time and a great door
is shut and stays shut against wind, sea, stone,
sunburst, and heavenfall. And home once more

inside the house of skin and struts of bone,
man-woman, woman-man, and each other,
I marry you by all dark and all dawn. . . . *

VARYING LEVELS OF ENERGY

The difference in sex is sometimes closely related to the difference in physical and emotional energy of two married people. Sometimes two people are more closely matched; both tire at about the same time; both have similar needs for rest and recreation. Sometimes the man will have the greater resources of energy, and sometimes it will be the woman.

You will want to learn about yourself and about each other. How much are you yourself able to do without tiring? How much can you both do together? How will you respond if you have to move at a slower

---

* From "*To Judith,*" by John Ciardi.

pace, or if you are expected to keep going beyond your natural strength?

As with any difference between you, you will want to be understanding and thoughtful of each other. You will want to avoid taxing each other with impossible physical demands, and at the same time you will want to do all you can to strengthen your marriage. The differences in energy can affect the recreation you share with each other, the games you play together, the vocational choices you make, the friends with whom you associate. In this area you will probably need a good bit of humor and a considerable willingness to compromise.

In the matter of sexual intercourse, for example, if there is a substantial difference in your levels of energy, you will need to be particularly thoughtful. One of you cannot demand sexual satisfaction when the other is physically exhausted without doing harm to your sex relationship. On the other hand, one of you cannot always be tired without doing similar damage. Together you can plan ahead, however, so that the less energetic one of you can try to get rested. You can arrange your sex life to match those times when both of you can participate in it fully.

TIMES FOR SELF-DENIAL

Sometimes in marriage a compromise is impossible, as sometimes in other areas of life you cannot have everything you want. Some compromises can destroy the integrity of the person who makes them. If you have talked things over, if you have examined yourself to make sure that you are being fair, if you still cannot find any satisfactory compromise, then it may be good for you to deny yourself what you want.

I know of a marriage, for example, which went on the rocks because the woman would not—or could not —curb her appetite for possessions. Her husband was making a good living, but not enough to support a wife with her extravagant tastes. If she saw a fur coat or a new piano, a designer hat, or fresh strawberries in February, she felt she had to have them all. Then she would berate her poor husband for not earning a large enough salary. Actually the trouble was in her, that she was unable to deny herself. Their marriage was reminiscent of the man who was reprimanded by a judge for deserting his wife. "Judge," he answered, "If you knew that woman as I do, you wouldn't call me a deserter. I'm a refugee."

Many times in marriage you will find it necessary to

curb your appetites and desires. You may have to deny your desire for sexual expression. You may have to curb your vacation plans to feed or clothe or educate your children. Your freedom may be cut down in various ways, but the joy of marriage is great enough that you can deny yourself ungrudgingly for the sake of harmony and your love for each other. If you can smile at yourself and laugh together, you will be learning that occasional self-denial is far more valuable than completely selfish freedom of action.

Practical Tips

Do things together which give you a chance to laugh together. Good humor needs frequent use.

Watch to see whether you are able to chuckle at your own foibles. The secret of a sense of humor lies in a person's capacity to be amused at himself.

Be ready to compromise for the sake of your marriage. The other person cannot, and should not, be asked to make all the concessions.

Accept, encourage and cherish the differentness of male and female contributions to your marriage.

Be prepared to deny yourself when insistence on your own way would weaken or ruin your marriage.

BOOKS ABOUT THE OCCASIONS FOR HUMOR AND COMPROMISE

LINDBERG, ANNE MORROW. *Gift from the Sea.* Pantheon Books, Inc., and New American Library of World Literature, Inc., New York.
A simple and moving series of reflections of a housewife. She takes time away from her family to rethink what they mean to her.

MONTAGU, ASHLEY. *The Natural Superiority of Women.* The Macmillan Company, New York.
Women will receive a boost to their morale from the argument of this book. The author says that they are physically stronger and emotionally more resilient than men. Male readers may be helped to receive appreciatively the peculiarly feminine contribution a wife can make.

WOOLF, VIRGINIA. *To the Light House.* Harcourt, Brace and Company, New York.
A masterpiece of novel writing. The woman in this marriage is endlessly giving. The man is the needful partner.

CHAPTER THREE:

Sex

IF IT were not for sex, marriage would soon drop out of existence. Sex is in the minds and on the lips of many crude humorists at the time of a wedding. Sex dominates the attention of many marriage counselors and fills the pages of most of the modern books about marriage. Sex talk is what most couples seem to expect when someone threatens them with premarital counsel. Let's admit it: sex is inextricably tied up with marriage.

Let's admit, further, that the humorists are on the trail of an important truth. Sex is a powerfully important instinct, and in our world it has been associated with all sorts of prohibitions, inhibitions and strange attitudes. Sex in marriage is a marvelous mixture of delicacy and strong animal drives, intimacy and social controls, the problem of unmatched moods and the desire to be close together. Sex can be the most confusing aspect of any marriage, and it can be one of the most wonderful and unifying. But many people, even in these supposedly enlightened days after Freud, find it hard to talk about sex without stammering and blushing under the surge of powerful feelings.

TWO FALSE VIEWS OF SEX

It is a serious thing for your marriage if you hold that sex is a dirty and unwholesome interest of which you must be ashamed. And yet, many people have been taught taboos on this subject. Starting with their own mother's teaching, they have learned that there must be something wrong about sex. They have been trained to seek sex information furtively and with an air of embarrassment. George Bernard Shaw, for example, the distinguished British playwright who was supposedly so emancipated, claimed that God created sex as a cruel joke upon the human race. Some persons have even been known to find the thought of sex so repulsive that they demand an advance agreement that the marriage will never be consummated by sexual union.

Now, of course, such people are extreme examples. But many people approach marriage with similar, taboo-filled attitudes toward sex. From their parents and from the church, at school and among their friends, they have learned to feel that sex is somehow evil and accompanied by guilt. As a result they are not free to let sex become the beautiful and unifying experience which it needs to be between a husband and wife.

Unfortunately the church itself has been responsible for a good share of the trouble in fostering this misleading attitude toward sex. For centuries the church has taught that sex is mysteriously associated with sin. And in this teaching, as we shall see in later sections, the church itself has ignored and misunderstood what the Bible says about the meaning of sex in marriage.

If you have a negative and inhibited view of sex, if you treat it as a sinful thing or as an unhappy necessity of human weakness, you can do great damage to your marriage. You can rob your marriage of the depth and wonder and mystery which sex should bring into the relation between husband and wife. It will be important for you to understand as deeply as you can why God

created you a sexual creature. Look honestly at your
God-given sexual capacity, and ask yourself what is
the proper meaning of sex in your marriage.

At the other extreme of the confusion which sur-
rounds sex is the approach of open exploitation. In this
view, sex is a kind of overwhelming animal drive. And,
if you want examples of this approach, you need to go
no further than the magazine display rack at the corner
drug store. On the covers of these magazines, you will
notice how sex is exploited to promote sales. And on
the inside pages, you will see how sex is being used to
peddle beer and ocean cruises, bathtowels and movie
stars.

On the surface, this approach may seem frank, honest
and appealing. It stresses the strength and urgency of
sexual desires. It makes physical pleasure seem a worthy
goal. It appears lusty and attractive. It can stir the deep
and passionate places of the imagination. It seems ad-
venturous, endlessly interesting and infinitely exciting.

Actually, however, this view of sex presents great
dangers to marriage. Its damage lies in the way it ignores
the depth of personal relationship which sex necessarily
involves. By exalting animal-like drives, it suggests that
sex can be casual, impersonal, promiscuous. But when
sex is used this way, it can end by destroying the person. It begins in a round of sexual adventures which be-

come increasingly meaningless. It then takes a person into restless disappointment, frustration, deepening loneliness and eventual despair. Used as a thing to be exploited, sex does in fact become degrading and sinful.

Your marriage, then, will need to steer a tricky course between the twin dangers of sexual exploitation and sexual inhibition. You ought to reckon with the power of sex and seek its beauty in marriage. Resisting every temptation to debase it, you will want to understand what sex can mean to you. And one of the best ways to understand how sex and marriage go together is to see what the Bible teaches on this subject.

SEX, LOVE, AND "ONE FLESH"

Two terms appear frequently in the Bible to describe the sexual relation between a man and a woman. And both terms suggest the tremendous meaning of sex union. Early in the stories about creation, for example, we come across this sentence: "Therefore shall a man leave his father and his mother, and shall cleave unto his wife: and they shall be one flesh" (Genesis 2:24).

That phrase "one flesh" appears many times in the Bible. It is found in the words of Jesus Christ and in the writings of the Apostle Paul. Wherever "one flesh" is used, it conveys the momentousness of the sexual relation. The term itself vividly suggests that the consequences of sexual intercourse permanently affect the life of two people who are involved. Even where the relation between them appears to be casual, or even where it is commercial, these consequences cannot be dismissed. Sex is one of the deepest forms of communication between two persons. It always leaves traces upon their lives. Whether these traces are to be good or evil depends upon the circumstances of the sexual union.

If, then, the subject of sex interests you, and if you believe it is significant for your marriage, biblical teaching can help you to understand its magnetic appeal. With profound realism the Bible shows that sex offers one of the most searching personal experiences a man or a woman can have. It engages the whole person—body, mind, heart and soul—and makes possible a union of depth and power. Sex probably reaches farther into the inner being of a man or a woman than any other aspect of our physical nature. Until you realize how fundamental sex is to your being, you will find it hard to take your sexual union with full seriousness. But when you grasp the Biblical teaching about "one flesh," you will find no other approach to the subject which does it full justice.

"Intercourse therefore is much more than a mere physical act which takes place on the periphery, as it were, of personal experience; it involves and affects the whole man and the whole woman in the very centre and depth of their being, so that afterwards neither can ever be as if they had never come together." [1]

There are many people with whom you can talk easily to pass the time of day. There are a few close friends with whom you can share experiences of great joy or sorrow. But in marriage you choose one person with whom to share your entire life. Words will not be able to convey all that you need to share with this person. There is no language, whether of speech or sign or even of silent understanding, which can express what you need to say. But in sexual intercourse God has given you a way to share the deepest things of your life with the other person. As you gain experience in your sexual relationship with each other, you will marvel at this language of love. You will thank God for making it possible for you to enter into a "one flesh" union.

Love is essential if any "one flesh" union is to be good rather than evil. (Have no doubt about it: sex is so deep and inclusive a feature of the human makeup that some kind of union takes place wherever there is a sexual transaction.) And sex gives you a way both to express and to stimulate your love for each other. It is always

[1] D. S. Bailey, *The Mystery of Love and Marriage*, pages 51-52. Harper & Brothers, New York. Used by permission.

possible, of course, to treat someone else as a thing to be used, an object of sensual pleasure, a source of security, or an agent of social status, rather than a person to be loved. But love cannot exist unless there is a personal relationship between the lovers. Each learns to see the other in increasingly personal ways. Each needs the other as a person to honor and cherish.

Such is the progress of love that it has to be profoundly, intimately personal. And in your union of "one flesh" through sexual intercourse you have a way to express and to share your love for each other. Love which has a language like this is able to grow deeper and more true. Sex, then, can help reveal you to each other.

"TO KNOW"

And this brings us to the second term which appears often in the Bible and has a wide range of meanings there. This is the verb "to know." Wherever this word occurs to describe the relationship between a man and a woman, it always refers to the sexual features of that relationship. So, for example, we read: "And Adam knew his wife, and she conceived, and bare Cain." And again we find that "Adam knew his wife again: and she bare a son, and called his name Seth." (Genesis 4:1 and 25.)

Like the phrase "one flesh," this word pictures the momentous consequences of sexual union. God has made sex to be a profoundly pervasive feature of human life. It expresses the entire person. It radiates out into every other instinct and interest. In the sex act one person not only comes "to know" another person, he learns "to know" himself.

". . . Through sexual intercourse man and woman come to understand the meaning of their masculinity and femininity and discover the solution to the enigma of personal existence. Why am I a man? Why am I a woman? . . . Only through the sexual act . . . can a man, as husband, reveal to a woman the secret of her womanhood, and a woman, as wife, reveal to a man the secret of his manhood . . . [This term] attains its full significance only when used of intercourse between husband and wife, who in 'knowing' one another also come to know themselves and the meaning of the mystery of sex." [2]

This is part of what the Bible teaches about sex in marriage. (The other part will be found in Chapter 4.)

[2] *The Mystery of Love and Marriage*, page 62.

It is a powerful, inclusive and potentially beautiful aspect of God's creation.

TECHNIQUE IN
LOVE-MAKING

Some people dislike the suggestion that technique is important in the sexual act. That makes the whole matter too mechanical, they feel. Sexual harmony, they argue, depends upon matching moods and tenderness and love. To pay attention to technique is to take away the warm spontaneity which should come first. And it is true that technical expertness by itself is not enough to provide your marriage with the most enduring joys of sexual harmony.

But it is also true that a bumbling, clumsy, misinformed approach to sex can damage your relationship, too. If your sexual information has been picked up from whispered school-corridor conversations or from the depths of your own uninformed imagination, then you need to know the facts, and you ought to know them accurately. Moreover, you ought to do enough reading about this subject so that, in your marriage, you can profit from the experience of other people and learn from their failures.

We have said that sexual intercourse is the language

of love. Technique is involved if you are to speak any language well. This certainly can be said, and said emphatically, about sex, where you need to learn the technique before you will be free enough to forget about technique as you speak this language with all its subtlety and nuance.

Many excellent books have been written about technique in the sexual act. You will find an annotated list of some of these books at the end of this chapter. You should read at least one of them before you marry. Look carefully at the diagrams, learn the proper terms, study about the different positions, understand what the sex act involves in a man and in a woman, and what moods are likely to arise before and after intercourse, so that you will be prepared realistically to use the sexual capacity which God has placed close to the center of your marriage. You will learn, in your developing experience together, the joy of "one flesh" union with the person you love.

Of course, you will also need a good physical examination before you marry. Many states now require a blood test before the marriage license is issued. But see to it that your physician does more than draw your blood. Have him examine your sex organs to make sure that you will have no physical handicap or pain. Ask questions about things you do not understand. Ask him to tell you of the proper use of lubricants. Think of asking him, too, for a fertility test: if it should turn out that you cannot have children, you should know before you marry. If you need minor, corrective surgery in order to have children, you will know the facts so that you can have it done. Request from him medically prescribed contraceptive materials, and information on how to use them. (You can, of course, buy contraceptives across the counter in many drug stores, but those prescribed by a doctor are both more safe and more comfortable.) Most doctors, however, are reticent about examining you carefully and making the necessary prescriptions. They wait for you to say you want their help, and then they can be very helpful. So the burden of seeking the information rests with you.

You may feel that you need more than physical advice. You may be mentally or emotionally unprepared for intercourse. Perhaps your mother taught you that it is an evil or unpleasant affair. Perhaps you find the thought of sex repugnant. Perhaps you have had an unfortunate experience with sex in childhood, or have guilty associations about it. In such a case, it may be well for you to speak frankly with your minister. He may suggest that you have a premarital interview with a good psychologist or psychiatrist or caseworker in a family service agency. Certainly you do not want to make your marriage limp along because of an attitude of yours which ought to be changed.

People sometimes wonder about the frequency of sexual intercourse in marriage. Should it occur only when children are wanted—as the church has sometimes seemed to teach? Or should it take place once a month or daily? The question is really one for you to decide. If we have been right so far about what the Bible teaches, then it follows that sex has another purpose besides procreation. It is meant as a deeply revealing and personal experience in marriage, when a husband and wife are united in a beautiful way. It is the expression of love, and it encourages stronger love. There is no special virtue, then, in sexual self-denial. Complete denial can, in fact, keep you from expressing love which you ought to be sharing. Love not expressed is frequently love growing cold or dying out. Very practically, too much sexual denial in your marriage can literally drive one of you into someone else's arms. So, be free with each other in your sexual give and take. Some happily married couples engage in intercourse approximately once a week. Others do it daily. In the early stages of their marriage, some couples find that intercourse occurs more frequently than it does later. In many happy marriages the sexual relationship continues to be important even into old age. Let your decision as to frequency, then, depend upon you—upon your levels of energy and your need to express your love—but do not allow your sexual relationship to lapse into complete disuse.

And if your sexual experience in marriage should seem unsatisfactory, get good advice promptly. After six months or a year, the basic sexual adjustments between a husband and a wife ought to have been made. The experience of intercourse ought to be welcome, satisfying and filled with deepening meaning. If, at the end of an initial period of experimentation and adjustment, you feel that you are not achieving the full expression of your love in "one flesh" union, then don't wait any longer. The matter is important enough to your marriage that you should get help without delay. Talk with your minister or find a good gynecologist, psychiatrist, psychologist or family case-worker, and try to free yourself for full participation in the sexual aspects of your marriage.

CHASTITY BEFORE MARRIAGE

The question is often raised by young people, "Is it important to stay chaste until marriage? Is there any harm in some sexual experience before I marry?" We have been saying that sex is a tremendously inclusive feature of a person's nature. It involves the whole person in a relationship of rare intimacy and sympathy. Any sexual intercourse, however casual or promiscuous, has lasting results. Any sex union between physically mature and reasonably intelligent people makes them, in biblical terms, "one flesh." They will never be the same for the experience they have shared together, nor will they ever again be quite apart from each other. Something of each sexual act will necessarily carry over into the ones which follow.

If, then, you treat the matter of chastity lightly, you are also treating the meaning of sex in marriage with similar lightness. Either you do not accept the depth and pervasiveness of the sexual relationship, or you do not value marriage as a profound and permanent relation between two people in love. If you understand how searching sexual union actually is, and if you cherish marriage as a high and holy calling, you will surely want to be chaste when you marry.

"But," people sometimes say, "we are in love. We are planning to marry. Is there any reason we should not have intercourse before our wedding day?" Apart from all the social and psychological reasons—such as uncomfortable and unpleasant surroundings, the fear of being caught, the fear of pregnancy, the guilt of anticipated disapproval—there is this reason: You may not marry after all. No one can ever be sure. Many marriages, firmly planned, have never taken place, and often for reasons not anticipated by the two most directly involved. Some have been cancelled right at the doors of the church. If you decide you cannot wait until you take your public vows, you will become "one flesh" with one another. And then, should anything happen to your marriage plans—like accidental death, let's say —you would have to carry into any other marriage the irrevocable fact that you were "one flesh" with someone else. No, it seems more sound, doesn't it, to wait until after your wedding day?

One more question does arise sometimes about chastity. It comes from a person who has already had premarital sexual experience, who for the first time has heard the biblical teaching about "one flesh," who senses intuitively that it is profoundly true, and who now wants to marry someone else. "What am I to do? How can I enter marriage now and keep it beautiful?" The question is hard because it is so yearning, so true to the basic facts of sex in the marriage relationship, and so sensitive to the needs of the other person.

If you are forced to ask this question, perhaps your best approach will be to seek the advice of a wise and experienced counselor. "One flesh," once established, remains, even though the love which prompted it is dead. It may remain a dead and evil fact, but it stays tied to you, inescapably a part of you. Perhaps you should seek the counsel of a minister, because penitence is the likeliest way for you to become free from the burden of your past. He can guide you in the penitential way. He can give you practical advice about the special problems you will face. He can encourage you and help you see when you are really ready for forgiveness. Then the fact of your past experience will remain, but you and your marriage will be freed from its burden.

SEXUAL FAITHFULNESS IN MARRIAGE

What we have been saying about chastity before marriage also applies in large part to sexual faithfulness within marriage. The God-given privilege of sexual union has abiding consequences in any human life. It unites two people irrevocably to each other. This union can either be good, becoming a basis for the rich harmony of married love, or it can be evil, wedding a person to guilt, frustration and eventual self-destruction. The meaning of sex in the divine design of creation is evident from the power of the sexual instinct, and from the way the sex act engages the whole person, whether or not he had expected to become fully involved. This meaning is emphasized by the realism and the seriousness of biblical teaching about sex.

So-called sexual "escapades," adventures, or "casual affairs" are, therefore, obviously impossible. Any act of sexual intercourse joins you as "one flesh" to the other person, whoever that person may be. For yourself there is real danger in any extra-marital affair which you may contemplate. By widening the range of your sexual relationships you thereby diminish the depth and power of your primary loyalty to your married mate. Furthermore, you deny an inescapable truth about your own nature. In diverting your sexual experience away from your marriage, you are perverting a capacity which could be good and creative. You are, in a real way, destroying yourself as effectively as a drunkard or a drug addict does. Your sexual appetite does not decrease; it may even increase. But your use of sex does not fill your own basic hungers. Instead, it deepens the emptiness in you and drives you into a widening series of sexual relationships. These expressions of your sexual need, far from satisfying you, only become increasingly impersonal and meaningless and frustrating. Unless you are reclaimed from the tightening chains of sexual promiscuity (and such reclamation is a painful ordeal) the final consequence of extra-marital sexual activity is destruction by despair.

And what you can do to yourself by unfaithfulness, you also do to your sexual partners and to your marriage. Your relationships become more and more trivial and impersonal. You begin to treat other persons as objects to be used for your pleasure and satisfaction, and in doing this you injure their personalities. Your marriage, of course, cannot long survive such a strain.

When you take the marriage vows, you agree, "forsaking all others," to keep you only to each other, "so long as ye both shall live." Clearly this part of the agreement applies primarily to the sexual relationship between you. In entering marriage with each other, you are rejecting everyone else as a potential marriage or sexual partner.

Actually your "forsaking" of all others turns out to be the positive choice of one person rather than a negative self-denial. And, curiously enough, your act of choosing a single partner frees you to form new kinds of relationship with the opposite sex. You will learn slowly during your marriage that you do not abandon these people. Rather, you have chosen one member of the other sex to be your partner in a union of "one flesh." And in making this choice you are freed from the compulsions and restraints of sex, freed to know men and women alike, as persons, whose sex is a diminishing fraction of their interest and importance to you.

Sexual promiscuity in extra-marital relations often develops slowly and unintentionally. Many husbands feel proud when other men are attracted to their wives, and many wives are flattered when other women try to flirt with their husbands. A certain amount of this teasing friendliness is natural, and possibly it is good for everyone's ego. Sexual unfaithfulness is more likely to occur when one person feels misunderstood or mistreated or has been sexually denied in the marriage bed. Unfaithfulness also occurs frequently when one person has started by trying to help someone of the opposite sex. The attempt may be completely sincere; but the reasons that we want to help someone else, especially of the opposite sex, are almost never pure. Sometimes the altruistic reasons we ascribe to our own behavior are simply a cover-up for our real subconscious intentions.

Marital infidelity, then, can surprise you and, perhaps, catch you off guard. If you develop patterns of infidelity, the results can be demonic in your own life and in your marriage. One way for you to meet the temptation to be unfaithful is to be cautious in forming intimacies with anyone of the opposite sex who is sexually attractive to you. Another is for you to maintain an open frankness with each other and to cooperate heartily in supporting each other. And perhaps the best way is for you to absorb deeply the biblical teaching about sex, so that you will want to reserve for your own marriage the mystery and the meaning of sexual love.

Practical Tips

Discuss with each other the implications for your marriage of the biblical teaching of "one flesh," so that you may be prepared to welcome your sexual union as an important and unifying feature of your life together.

Read enough literature on this subject so that you will understand the facts of sex and will be prepared to experiment with this language of love.

When you see your doctor, make sure that both of you are examined to ascertain your physical readiness for intercourse. Minor disabilities can create discomfort in the sex act and can often be corrected easily before marriage.

Ask your doctor for the proper contraceptive equipment and information before you marry. This is important (see Chapter 4 about children) so that you can be free in your early sexual experiences with each other.

Be prepared to enter your sexual union without inhibition and with a full readiness to experiment. The language of sexual intercourse can be extremely varied, and you should be ready to allow it fully to express your love for each other.

Approach your sexual life from the very beginning with an attitude of tenderness and thoughtfulness towards each other. If it is to be an adequate expression of your married love, sex must become equally meaningful and satisfying to each of you.

Questions about sex are likely to arise in your minds after you have been married for a while. Do not hesitate to get accurate information and counsel as soon as you need it, either from a book or from a competent professional advisor.

Books About Sex in Marriage

Butterfield, Oliver M. *Sex Life in Marriage*. Emerson Books, Inc., New York.
An excellent, full-length introduction to this subject. Complete, competent, thoughtful. For those who want *all* the facts.

Stone, Hannah and Abraham. *A Marriage Manual*. Simon and Schuster, Inc., New York.
Another authoritative book which deals almost entirely with sexual subjects.

DAVIS, MAXINE. *The Sexual Responsibility of Woman.* Dial Press, Inc., New York.

A brightly written, helpful treatment of the meaning of sex in marriage, from the physical, social and psychological point of view. Intended mainly to help the woman understand herself and her husband.

BAILEY, D. S. *The Mystery of Love and Marriage.* Harper & Brothers, New York.

An essay which develops in greater detail the point of view of this chapter. The approach is theological. The language is somewhat technical.

BUTTERFIELD, OLIVER M. *Sexual Harmony in Marriage.* Emerson Books, Inc., New York (available in pamphlet and gift edition).

One of the best brief treatments of the physical and emotional features of sex. Readable, accurate, sensible. I give a copy to every couple I marry.

CHAPTER FOUR:

Children

MARTIN LUTHER, a confirmed bachelor during the first eight years of the German Reformation, finally agreed to marriage. Somewhat reluctantly and at the urging of his closest friends, he decided to marry Katherine von Bora. Later he confided to an associate, "There is a lot to get used to in the first year of marriage. One wakes up in the morning and finds a pair of pigtails on the pillow which were not there before." [1]

You will discover the truth of Luther's comment dur-

[1] Quoted by Roland Bainton, *Here I Stand*, page 290.

ing your first year of life together. It is a year of many adjustments, some of them wonderfully delightful, and some perplexing. It is a year of unfolding sexual intimacy, a year when you are setting the patterns of your marriage, a year when you are planning together for your first baby. You need this time for yourselves, so that you can be free to make your own delicate adjustments to marriage. It can be a period of great fun, deepening affection and rapid personal growth.

At the end of this period, which cannot last very long, you will be ready to welcome new members into the family you have planned. And then you will learn the other great reason for sex union in marriage: children. Through the sex relation you take part together in creating a new life. In the sex act you actually share with God the divine work of creation. Your child is the visible embodiment of your union of "one flesh." Your baby is the two of you, indivisibly bound together in a new and unique person. And this child is the creation of your common love, the living summary of your past union and the projection into the future of all your loving hopes. Having a child is one of the fundamental privileges of marriage and is the culmination of the mystery of your sexual relationship.

But every child born into the world has a right to be welcome and wanted. You should be reluctant to bring children into a marriage if you are not ready to receive them with joy. This, of course, is one reason for the use of contraceptives. In the early period of your marriage, contraception assures you the opportunity to explore and to experiment in your sexual relation with each other. As we have seen in the previous chapter, children are not the only purpose of sex. Sex has a fundamental purpose in uniting a husband and wife in the harmony of married love. Children are the culminating purpose of sex, but not its only reason. Children are love made visible. In justice to them they deserve to be wanted and properly spaced so that they can receive adequate love and care. Children ought not to be accidents that "just happened." They need to be planned for, prayed for, cared about and loved.

GETTING READY FOR YOUR BABY

Early in your life together, then, you will begin to make plans about your children—how many children you will have, how they will be spaced, and how they will be raised. Perhaps you will also want to plan such impossible angles as how many of your children will be boys and how many girls! Probably you will be wondering, too about such practical questions as how much money you should have saved before you begin your family.

Some couples enter marriage with a burden of financial debts which needs to be cleared away before they have any children. Others will wish to wait until a lengthy period of graduate education is completed. In such marriages it may be necessary to wait as long as three years for the first child. But usually a couple will be ready within six months or a year to try to have a baby. Few people ever have enough money to guarantee security and an educational future for their children. If you wait too long, the reason may be selfishness on your part, or misunderstanding of what a child really needs. Your family does not require luxury or vast expense. What your children need most is you, and the knowledge that you want them and love them. As soon as your relationship to each other is well started and secure, you ought to become parents.

Sometimes, however, this is easier said than done. Any child is a gift from God, and not something automatic which you alone can cause to happen. The miraculous nature of this gift becomes clear as you share the marvels of pregnancy and become aware of the stirrings of new life and participate in the drama of birth. God may make a surprise of this gift by giving you a baby when you had not planned for one, or by making you wait much longer than you had expected. Sometimes the gift of a child is denied altogether to a marriage. Then the preciousness and the poignancy of this gift is heightened.

If you find that you cannot have a baby—after you have tried and have received the best medical advice available—see if you can adopt a child. A good family or children's casework agency can be a great help to you. Often children placed in adoptive homes can be ideally matched to the parents, though usually the plans for adoption take a long time. And the parents always gain from the experienced advice of people who know what it means to become an adoptive parent.

Of course, you will find great joy in getting ready for your baby, whether it comes naturally or by adoption. You will prepare the clothes and fit out the baby's tiny bed. You will read about children and talk about them with your friends. If you have had no experience with new babies, you will want to get acquainted with some. The father especially ought to visit the nursery of the nearest hospital, so that he can be prepared for the tiny, wrinkled, red-faced, screaming child with which his wife is likely to present him. Many fathers know that a new-born baby cannot be expected to play baseball, but men are notoriously unrealistic about this subject. Often they show surprise—and sometimes disappointment—when they first see their own child. Naturally, such disappointment is an affront to the triumphant mother.

You will also want to make spiritual preparations for your child. If the religious directions and loyalties of your marriage have been put off, they must no longer be neglected. This is the time to choose your common church home and to plan where your baby will be baptized. It is also the time for you to develop the religious practices within your home, to talk together about God's movements and actions within your marriage, to establish the periods when you will pray and study the Bible together. Then you will be ready to thank God for his gift of children, to lift up to God your hopes and anxieties during the period of pregnancy, and when your baby finally arrives, you will be able to offer a home where faith is growing and where prayer is a natural and wholesome feature of the common life.

WHEN YOUR BABY COMES

When your baby does come, you will lavish all kinds of attention and affection upon it. You will stand wonderingly over the crib, watching the small movements of the child asleep and listening anxiously for the sounds of breathing and the signs of life. Your baby will seem so improbable and yet so perfect down to the tiniest fingernail, so delicate and so helpless that you will be zealous in its care and protection.

But you will also be learning the meaning of trust. Unless you are to become exhausted by the strain of an impossible round-the-clock vigil at the crib, you will have to learn how to trust your child's life to God. After you have done everything that you can do, you will need to be able to say a prayer of thanksgiving and of loving petition, such a prayer as this one: "So fill our hearts with trust in Thee that by night and by day, at all times and in all seasons, we may without fear commit those who are dear to us to Thy never-failing love for this life and the life to come. Amen."

One development which surprises many new parents is the bone-weary tiredness they feel. A tiny baby may not look like much trouble, but it can cause you to lose a lot of sleep. When it cries to be fed or changed in the middle of the night, or when its many dirty clothes have to be laundered, or when it keeps you awake for no apparent reason, or because it is sick, you will be finding that even the smallest baby can demand a lot of attention and love. You will want to work out ways of overcoming your tiredness—perhaps you will need to take turns on the midnight shift

—so that you will be alert enough to love your child and enjoy it.

Many parents also need to be prepared for another kind of development. Often, after birth, the mother suffers what the doctors call a "postpartum depression." In some cases this depression can be very serious, and it usually appears in some degree with every birth. What it means is that the mother feels drained, exhausted and depressed after she has had the baby. Frequently this depression comes just when she thinks she should be recovering her health and should be elated to have a healthy child. She cannot understand her own moods and feels helpless in trying to improve them. The doctors now believe that the postpartum depression results from complex chemical changes which are taking place in the mother's body. Her whole body gradually adjusted throughout the pregnancy to supporting an additional life. Now, however, that life has suddenly become independent of her, and she has had to go through many glandular adjustments to regain her normal pace of life. If both of you understand and are ready for the development of this depression, you can be better prepared to cope with it when it does come.

YOUR CHILD GROWS

It is never too early for you to begin to talk about how you will train your children. Will they be raised exactly as your own parents raised you? Or will you combine your parents' approach with some new twists of your own? Or will your children be brought up in a radically different way? Out of such a conversation you will be evolving your theories of child-care long before you have to apply them to your own children. And you will be getting ready to stand together against those people who insist that your theories are wrong. Of course, there are many, and sharply conflicting, views of how children should be brought up. Whether you are going to be strict disciplinarians or totally permissive parents, you can be sure that someone will disagree with you.

Clucking neighbors, anxious relatives and zealous friends will be ready to offer advice, much of it unwanted and unwelcome. When they begin to shake their heads ominously and make crystal clear their conviction that your approach is wrong, they may be able to shake your confidence in yourselves as parents. (For more details on how to handle relatives and friends, see Chapter 7.) Because you will be new to parenthood, it will be important for you to stand firmly together. Your children will need consistent treatment from you. If you have planned your approach to child-raising, you can weather outside pressures and find great joy in watching your children grow.

Several of the books which are listed at the end of this chapter are worth buying, and you should have them for ready reference in your home. They are practical, common sense books. They can tell you what is normal child behavior in the various age groups. They can comfort and encourage you as you meet views which oppose your own. These books are based upon wide experience and the observation of many different children. Especially as you wonder how to handle your first child, books like these can mean a great deal to you.

And if, for any reason, you should want advice which the books do not give, you can find expert professional advisors almost everywhere. The larger cities usually have excellent Child Guidance Clinics or Children's Service Associations. At these places you can find experienced people to help you understand your children.

In the beginning you may feel that you are giving a great deal to your children. You are planning for their future; you are accepting responsibility for their welfare; you are giving yourselves to their daily care. But at some point you will realize how much your children are giving to you. They will return your love. They will have their own ways of showing how much they need and appreciate you. They will contribute humor and zest and breadth to your marriage. As they grow, you will marvel at their unfolding personalities, and you will be glad you have had a share in the creation of such distinct human beings.

Then, you yourselves will grow. Your marriage will be transformed and rounded out to meet one of its greatest purposes. You will be becoming a true family. And you will thank God for the marvelous and mysterious blessing which children have brought into your home.

Practical Tips

Begin now to talk about how you will raise your children, finding the approach upon which you two can stand together even though other people may frown upon it.

Before your first baby is born, let the father go to the nursery window of the hospital and ask the nurse to show him several new-born babies. He ought to know what to expect.

Get some good books which describe, in detail, the normal stages of a child's development and study them together.

It is always better for you to ask help from good child guidance counselors before a child's problems are deep-rooted in the child's personality.

Remember that normal children need two parents working closely together. To stay closely together, you will need to plan times when you can develop your relationship to each other. If you allow it, your children will absorb all your time, including that which you ought to spend together. You may need to arrange an occasional overnight trip when you get away from your family, to have a good time together and develop new perspectives on your joint role as parents.

Remember this word from a distinguished psychologist, "A man's first duty to his children is to keep their mother happy."

Books About Children

Spock, Benjamin. *Common Sense Book of Baby and Child Care*. Duell, Sloan & Pearce, Inc., New York (also available in a very popular Pocket Book edition).
A baby doctor, with a lively pen and a comforting approach, tells how a baby behaves and why. Particularly useful with the first baby.

GESELL, ARNOLD, and ILG, FRANCES. *Infant and Child in the Culture of Today*. Harper & Brothers, New York.
An authoritative and useful book on child development. Tells what to expect at the different stages of a child's developments by describing typical "Behavior Days" of an average child.

CLEVELAND, ANNE. *The Parent from Zero to Ten*. Simon and Schuster, Inc., New York.
An amusing book of cartoons and commentary, purporting to give the typical "Behavior Days" of average parents. Good for anyone who enjoys a laugh. Necessary for all parents who plan to be somberly "scientific" in child raising.

CHAPTER FIVE:

Money does matter

A FOUR-YEAR-OLD acquaintance of mine has recently made a practice of discovering dimes. Where he finds these ten-cent pieces his parents are not able to guess, perhaps in a piggy bank, perhaps in his mother's purse, perhaps he keeps discovering the same coin over and over again. At any rate, he rushes up to his parents, clutching a dime in his little fist and shouting, "Look! See! I found a penny!"

The joyous discoveries of that small boy suggest some features of the financial problem that may arise in your marriage. The value of money is not simply what the government stamps on the face of a coin. The important value is what you attribute to it.

Some adults treat money carelessly, as though a dime had only the value of a penny.

Some value money highly, scrupulously guarding the smallest coins.

Some people lavishly spend all their income, while others strive to pile up savings.

Some use money as a provider of pleasure, while others see it as a source of security.

Some dream of owning vast sums of money, while others frankly do not want to be bothered with riches at all.

For many people money is valued neither for itself alone nor for what it will buy, but as a mark of status and a source of power.

Because such wide differences of opinion do exist as to the value and the use of money, you will need to spend a great deal of time discussing with each other the place of money in your marriage. You may think in a general way that you are completely agreed already, but specific questions may reveal margins of difference which you had not suspected. Should you buy a washing machine or a new car, a deep freeze or an outboard motor? Should you get seats for a concert series or make a contribution to the church? As you decide such questions as these, differences in your values may emerge.

The use of money can introduce cold, impersonal selfishness into marriage. Money can be used as a tool by which one person tries to dominate the other. Feelings can run very deeply in financial disagreements.

The purpose of this chapter, then, is to introduce you to some of the ways that money can matter in marriage. It is intended to start a financial conversation between you before you marry. By dealing with specific, practical questions now, you can begin to lay down the principles which will govern your money matters for the future. As you take time now to discuss in detail the questions raised in this chapter, you will be making possible a fruitful conversation on this subject for years to come. Money, like everything else in marriage, becomes a most serious problem when a frank and honest exchange of opinions about it no longer seems possible.

ABOUT BUDGETS

Many people marry before they have had personal financial responsibility for their own lives. They have been dependent upon their parents for almost everything right up to their wedding day. They have only the vaguest ideas about the cost of food and housing, transportation and medical care. They realize dimly that money has a peculiar way of going out faster than it comes in, but they have had neither training nor experience in its management.

The purpose of the much-misunderstood family budget is to help you manage your money according to your own intelligent plan, rather than according to your fleeting impulses. For most couples a budget is a great aid to financial survival and to matrimonial harmony. As you gain experience in planning and keeping a budget, you will be able to make your money work for you instead of being dominated by it.

For example, you may have some small indulgences which seem like minor expenses to you, such things as chewing gum or eating candy, smoking or buying a daily cup of coffee. If you stop to do some basic arithmetic, you will see that ten cents a day amounts to $36.50 a year. Then you will have to ask yourself whether your favorite indulgence is really worth that much money to you, or would you prefer to save the money for some other use.

Several basic principles govern the effective use of a family budget. The first is that you make a long-range, annual estimate of both your expenses and your expenditures. Then you can divide your annual estimate into smaller divisions as they may be convenient for you. The advantage of the long-range plan is that many of your expenses occur only occasionally, perhaps only once or twice a year. If you have not thought ahead to these expenses and prepared for them, you may be caught with insufficient funds to meet them. Your estimated budget, then, might look something like this:

★ ANTICIPATED INCOME (From all sources)	MONTHLY	YEARLY
I. Salary or Wages	$ - - - · - -	$ - - - - · - -
II. Investments	- - - · - -	- - - - · - -
III. Gifts	- - · - -	- - - · - -
IV. Other	- - · - -	- - - · - -
Totals	$ - - - · - -	$ - - - - · - -

★ ANTICIPATED EXPENSES

I. Housing		
a) *Rent or Mortgage*	$ - - - · - -	$ - - - - · - -
b) *Utilities*	- - - · - -	- - - - · - -
c) *Furnishings*	- - · - -	- - - · - -
	$ - - - · - -	$ - - - - · - -

★ ᴀɴᴛɪᴄɪᴘᴀᴛᴇᴅ Exᴘᴇɴsᴇs	Mᴏɴᴛʜʟʏ	Yᴇᴀʀʟʏ
II. Food	$ - - - - · - -	$ - - - - · - -
III. Clothing		
a) *Husband*	$ - - · - -	$ - - - · - -
b) *Wife*	- - · - -	- - - · - -
	$ - - - - · - -	- - - · - -
IV. Medical		
a) *Drugs*	$ - - · - -	$ - - · - -
b) *Dentist*	- - · - -	- - · - -
c) *Doctors*	- - · - -	- - · - -
d) *Hospitalization*	- - · - -	- - · - -
	$ - - · - -	$ - - · - -
V. Transportation		
a) *Purchase of car*	$ - - · - -	$ - - - - · - -
b) *Running Expenses*	- - · - -	- - - · - -
c) *Insurance and*		
Taxes	- - · - -	- - · - -
d) *Repairs*	- · - -	- - · - -
	$ - - - · - -	$ - - - - · - -
VI. Insurance and Savings		
a) *Insurance*		
Premiums	$ - - · - -	$ - - - - · - -
b) *Savings*	- - · - -	- - - · - -
	$ - - · - -	$ - - - · - -

★ ANTICIPATED EXPENSES   MONTHLY   YEARLY

VII. Personal Allowances
    a) *Husband* $ - - . - - $ - - - . - -
    b) *Wife*   - - . - -   - - - . - -
    c) *Gift Allowances*   - . - -   - - . - -
                          $ - - . - - $ - - - . - -

VIII. Philanthropy
    a) *Church* $ - - . - - $ - - - . - -
    b) *United Fund*   - . - -   - - . - -
    c) *Others*   - . - -   - - . - -
                          $ - - . - - $ - - - . - -

IX. Recreation and
   Education
    a) *Vacations* $ - - . - - $ - - - . - -
    b) *Books and*
       Magazines   - . - -   - - . - -
    c) *Movies, Plays,*
       Sports   - . - -   - - . - -
    d) *Entertain Friends*   - . - -   - - . - -
                          $ - - . - - $ - - - . - -

★ ANTICIPATED EXPENSES   MONTHLY   YEARLY

X. Taxes
    a) *Income Tax* $ - - . - - $ - - - . - -
    b) *State Taxes*   - - . - -   - - . - -
    c) *Other*   - - . - -   - - . - -
        Total $ - - . - - $ - - - . - -
        Expenses $ - - - . - - $ - - - - . - -

Of course, you will have to make sure that the total of your estimated expenses does not exceed your total estimated income. If it does, then you will need to cut some of the things on which you wanted to spend money. Some couples find that their differences in values show up most vividly when they are trying to decide where to whack away at their expenses. You will discover also, that with several years of experience, you can estimate your expenses with increasing precision. In time, you will want to include the cost of children in your estimates. Food, clothing, medical care, education and sometimes housing are all items which increase with each child. Remember always that your budget is not a tyrant running your life. Its whole purpose is to help you, within your means, to live the kind of a life that you want.

A second basic principle about family budgets is that you keep complete records of *everything* you spend. Even what may seem like a small expenditure to you can mount up over the course of a year, so that if it is not recorded, it can upset your entire budget. Most bookstores and stationery stores have simple ledger books which can help you to keep your accounts accurately. These records, honestly kept, can give you a realistic guide to your own financial life. They can help you eliminate those expenses you do not really care about, and they can show you how to afford those things you truly want.

For example, you ought to include in your budget money for those activities which will draw you together as a couple (see Item IX in the budget suggested above) such things as trips, movies, plays, concerts, dancing, dinners. If, by stinginess, you have not been fair to your own marriage, the budget record will remind you that it is time to spend money having a good time together. If however, you have a tendency to spend too much money on such activities, the budget will warn you to be careful. As you record the money you have already spent, the figures themselves may persuade you that it is time for you to pull in your belts and stay at home more frequently.

A third basic principle about budgets is that you allow

money to accumulate under certain categories instead of transferring it to another item. If, for example, you have not spent what you had budgeted for medical expense, that is no reason for spending the money for something else. You have just been blessed with good health. You will need to save that money against the day when you may have heavy medical costs. Allow it to accumulate until the need arises for which you had budgeted the money.

There are, of course, other ways of planning and keeping budgets in addition to the one suggested above. You may have special problems, not mentioned here. You may want to try another approach. You may want advice on what proportion of your income should go for housing and what proportion for savings. You may need expert help in setting up your first budget. A caseworker in a family service agency can be very helpful to you. The federal and state governments make frequent studies which may be of some use. Chambers of Commerce and Taxpayers' Associations have helpful information. Some ministers, lawyers, certified public accountants and investment counselors have made themselves expert enough to be of real assistance. If you yourselves have not had much experience in handling money, you will be smart to seek the advice of someone in your own community. Several additional books have been suggested at the end of this chapter. But remember that your budget will vary depending upon your income, the cost of living in your part of the country, and the ways you both agree to use your money. Talking directly to someone who understands these matters may be the wisest course you can take.

BANKS, INSURANCE AND SAVINGS

Do you plan to have a joint account at the bank or separate accounts, or do you expect to stash your money away in an old sock under the mattress? A bank, of course, is the safest place for you to keep your money. And if you pay most of your bills by check, you can use the mails easily and will have a complete record of receipts. Whether or not you have joint or separate accounts will depend upon such factors as how much you will be sharing the responsibility in your home, whether you are equally good at arithmetic, and what arrangement is more convenient for you.

Incidentally, it may be a good idea to look up the laws in your state concerning death and inheritance. Sometimes a bank account gets tied up in probate court procedures, and a new widow is caught for months without access to any money.

Whatever method of banking you may choose, the woman's needs ought to be remembered particularly. If she is not going to work and has no other sources of personal income, she needs to have ready access to the family funds. She should receive an allowance regularly and routinely for running the house. She should never, through thoughtlessness, be made to appear nagging as she tries to get money to pay the household bills. Some money should always go straight to the housekeeper.

Moreover, each of you needs a small personal allowance (see budget Item VII a and b). This is money which you may use foolishly and frivolously if you wish. It is money for which you will not have to account to each other. Certain areas of privacy belong in every marriage. These private domains actually nourish the marriage. The joy of being together is enhanced and enriched if they are respected. So, whatever your banking plan, arrange to give each other a degree of financial privacy.

A bank is not only a place to keep your money safely. It is also a place to assist you in a regular plan for saving money. What you deposit in a savings account is somewhat harder to take out than the money in a checking account. Therefore, you are more likely to save it. Moreover, through interest payments, your savings money can be earning you modest sums of additional money.

For many middle-income families, however, life insurance is the best and safest form of savings, and it provides protection in case of death as well. More and more insurance policies are being written with annuity programs in them, which means that a steady, supplemental income is assured when you retire.

Three things are important for you to remember about life insurance. First of all, it is cheaper for you to buy it now than it will ever be again. For each year of your age the price of an equivalent amount of insurance goes up. Second, you are always worth more alive than dead. If you estimate your average annual earnings at $5,000 and your probable working life at forty years, then your dollar value is $200,000, much more money than you can afford to guarantee through insurance. But you can afford enough to be a real help to your wife and your dependents in case of your death. In the third place, a good life insurance program offers as much protection in case you should live as if you should die. The annuity feature of an insurance policy can make the difference between comfort and indigence when you retire.

Recently the insurance world has become immensely

complicated. Of course, you will need to agree with each other on the broad outlines of what you want to do. Then you should look up a reliable insurance salesman and ask him to advise you. If you do not know a salesman whom you can trust, here are two suggestions to help in your selection. First get someone who is attached to a well-known and reputable company. Second, get someone who can write C. L. U. (Chartered Life Underwriter) after his name. Those letters are like a business pedigree, indicating that the holder is ethical and is specially trained in the complexities of modern insurance. Such a person can tailor a plan to fit your special needs.

CREDIT AND BORROWING

Another matter, closely related to budget-making, is the question of credit and borrowing. A family that buys everything from the kitchen chairs to the children's toys "on time" is borrowing needless trouble and adding unnecessary tensions to the marriage. To be sure, much retail trade in our country rests heavily upon credit buying, and the bewitching blandishments of the stores may seem hard to resist, but lax use of credit can wreak havoc in a home and unleash bickering, self-seeking acquisitiveness.

Plan carefully, then, and be wary how you use credit. Most middle-income families need to borrow money for their house and, frequently, for their car. Beyond that, they may keep several charge accounts open (and paid up regularly!). But with any additional heavy expenses, they will try to plan ahead of time and save for them through use of the budget. They know that high interest rates make money one of the most expensive things in the world to buy. They would prefer to have their money earning interest in a savings bank, rather than costing interest as they plod wearily through payments on a loan.

If you are forced for some reason to borrow money, make sure that you get the facts and the best possible advice. The most expensive place you can go for money is also the easiest—a small loan company. The interest rates there run as high as 36 per cent and repayments will be terribly hard. Next in line is the small loan department of a commercial bank. Curiously enough, your money costs less dollar for dollar, if you borrow a large amount at the bank. Before you borrow, however, you should do the arithmetic, or have someone else do it, so that you can see exactly what the loan will cost you. The lowest interest rates you get will probably be where you can offer an insurance policy, your home, or other valuable property as collateral.

SHOULD WIVES WORK?

Another matter concerning finances for you to discuss before your marriage is whether the wife should work. Some men, Central Europeans for instance, come from a cultural background where the man is supposed to be the breadwinner. It is a direct affront to his ability and, therefore, to his manhood, if his wife works. Increasingly in our country, however, wives are going to work and their work raises questions about which you need to think together.

Many women, in the first years of marriage, want to work. They put their earnings into kitchen furnishings, buying a house and rainy-day savings. It makes them feel, they say, that they have made a tangible contribution to the building of their home. And, in their later years, if they are fortunate enough to get work, many women enjoy building up resources for their retirement.

The real rub about working wives seems to come when the children are growing up. And here you will have to make a financial decision of great significance. Two considerations are important. First, do you really need the money which the wife earns, or do you just think you need it? There is quite a difference between need and desire. For many Americans this difference has become fuzzy, but where the welfare of children is involved, you will do well to make it clear.

Second, is the wife working in order to escape the monotony of the house and in order to get into the more interesting world of business? You have probably heard women many times identify their vocation as "just housewife." That deprecating word "just" reveals the low opinion many women hold of their own calling. Surely it is true that few activities can get more dull than the daily rounds of dusting, laundry, dirty dishes, carried on in the midst of the din of childrens' voices. But few jobs on earth are more important than those performed by a dependable and loving mother. The husband needs to recognize his wife's crucial role: that the adults in the next generation are being moulded today by her. What she does every day is probably more important to the future world than the work that he is doing. A husband can constantly remind his wife of his own firm belief that her work in the home is as important as his own. He can do a great deal to support her through the most difficult years of child raising. Children need to have their mother constantly available. No other arrangement is an adequate substitute. But the mother needs frequent and sincere reassurances from her husband that her work is significant.

YOU AND PHILANTHROPY

An altogether different kind of question needs your discussion and agreement. This is your program of philanthropy. Remember that marriage has a social significance beyond the relationship of two individuals who have fallen in love. A good marriage is a blessing in any community, and a bad one is a curse upon it. Conversely, a decadent community is a handicap to any home, while an alert and civic-minded community will strengthen it. You are not simply marrying each other. The quality of your life together will influence many other lives and will, in turn, be affected by the character of the community in which you live.

It is of the highest importance, then, that you strive to support the finest possible churches and schools, libraries and juvenile courts and social agencies. These institutions mould the civic and social influences which will affect your marriage. You will want the best for your family, and the best will require your generous financial support.

When you start to discuss with each other what proportion of your income you will give to the church and to social welfare, you may be in for a surprise. Both of you may agree that you want to be generous.

But when you talk about specific amounts, what seems generous to one of you may seem downright miserly to the other. Money has a strange way of bringing our basic differences of opinion into focus.

TOO MUCH OR TOO LITTLE?

During the exchange of your vows in the marriage service, you will promise to take each other "for richer for poorer." The phrase may have little meaning for you right now. Your temptation may be to believe that your love can overcome the most stubborn and practical obstacles. And so it may! But love needs the undergirding of clear planning and mutually agreeable goals. You cannot determine positively how much or how little money you will have. But you can be talking about how much you want to have. Money is sure to play an important part in your marriage. Do you dream of owning a lot of money, or do you want just enough to meet your basic needs, or haven't you thought about your financial future?

A curious fact about money is that it can cause problems regardless of the amount that you have. Obviously, when there is not enough money there is the haunting anxiety of how to pay the bills, such as the pinched threadbare quality that comes into your life together when even a prescription for penicillin is a blow to the budget. In very poor homes financial anxiety can be constant worry and can rob marriage of much of its joy.

But too much money can raise other kinds of difficulties. If, for example, you are already wealthy as you enter marriage, your money can raise barriers to the process of mutual sharing which is so important to marriage. You may be willing to give your heart away when you marry, and your body, and your private dreams. But sharing your purse may be something else again. Unless you are extremely cautious and a very mature person you may come to use your money with a club-and-carrot technique to coerce your partner. Similarly, if you gain access to great wealth after you marry, you may be catapulted into a new and unfamiliar world. There are many dangers in too much money. Subtle changes in your values may create friction between you, and the knowledge of your wealth may come between you, making you feel increasingly independent of each other.

What is too much and what is too little? The question is hard, and you will not find any ready answers to it. The wise and far-seeing realism of the marriage service would have you ready to meet either extreme. It would have you concentrate on maintaining your marriage instead of being diverted by the quest of riches. When you take each other "for richer for poorer," you are saying that you will not be dominated by financial dreams. You will handle your money sensibly and gratefully, whether you have much or little. You may be promising fifty years into the future as you say those words. Perhaps your best ambition about money will be to have enough for comfort and no more.

ON BECOMING STEWARDS

One teaching of the Christian church has been a great help to many couples as they have wrestled with the problems associated with money. This teaching is called stewardship. Briefly stated stewardship rests on the belief that everything we possess is actually a gift from God.

> He gives and sustains our life.
> He gives us all our talents.
> He makes it possible for us to have food and clothes,
>   to earn money
>   to use the natural resources of the world around
>   us.
> He allows us the precious gift of time.

Nothing we possess, then, is ours by natural or inalienable right. A popular adage states the real situation accurately, "You can't take it with you." Everything we have is, you might say, loaned to us temporarily from a store that belongs eternally to God.

Our task, therefore, is to learn to become good stewards of the treasures which God has allowed us to use. We can learn to use the gifts of time and money and talent in ways that are pleasing to God and satisfying to us. We can become relaxed about the driving desires of possession. We can become free enough to use our possessions wisely, instead of allowing them to use us. We can express our gratitude to God in the way we treat his gifts to us.

The real question, then, is not how much or how little money you expect to have. The important question for you to settle early in your marriage is how you will use what God has given you. If you learn to be good stewards, many of the most haunting financial problems will never even arise for you.

Practical Tips

Before you marry, get someone to help you set up a budget and to show you the way to keep your accounts. Especially if neither of you has had experience with money, make sure that you get expert help on your first budget.

Include in your budget something for those activities that draw you together as a couple (see page 69).

If the wife is not going to work, make sure that she receives regularly and routinely an allowance for running the house.

If you feel you have to borrow money, do so cautiously and after you have figured its real cost and have received the best advice available.

Agree, before you marry, whether the wife will work after you have children. What age should the children be before she works? What use will be made of the money she earns?

Discuss what your approach to philanthropy will be. The reasons you give to charitable causes can be more important than the amounts you give.

Learn from your church something of the meanings of Christian stewardship. See whether this teaching of the church can be applied helpfully to the financial aspects of your marriage.

BOOKS ABOUT FAMILIES AND FINANCES

LASSER, J. K. and PORTER, SYLVIA. *Managing Your Money*. Henry Holt and Company, Inc., New York.
A simple, readable and inclusive guide to family finances by two well-known writers on financial subjects.

TAYLOR, ELIZABETH. *A View of the Harbor*. Alfred A. Knopf, Inc., New York.
A controversial novel about what happens when a woman puts her career first.

Woolson's Economy Expense Book. Samuel Ward Manufacturing Company, Boston.
An example of a home account ledger book, with instructions on how to use it.

Government Printing Office, Washington, D. C.
An up-to-date and inexpensive list of pamphlets on finances is always available at this source.

The Household Finance Corporation, Research Department, Chicago, Ill.
Current pamphlets on family financing: A practical and very helpful selection of materials.

CHAPTER SIX:

What if we disagree?

THE wife of an internationally-renowned minister was being interviewed on a popular television show. The interviewer pounced on her with this question:

"Do you and your husband ever disagree or argue?"

The lady thought for just a moment. Then she quietly replied:

"My husband and I feel that where two people always agree, one of them is unnecessary."

Perhaps the hardest thing for you to believe about

your marriage is summed up in her retort. *You will have differences of opinion.* As long as you live together you will not always agree. Either that, or else one of you will become unnecessary. Of course, you don't have to resolve your differences by throwing saucepans. But you do need to be ready to cope with disagreements.

The secret of married harmony lies in the way you handle your disagreements, in the spirit with which you approach the strained situations that arise between you. During your courtship you have learned that it doesn't really help to be angry with each other, or to refuse to speak to each other, or to say disrespectful things to each other. You have learned that the most wonderful thing about love is that it can pull two people together in spite of differences of opinion. Indeed, love often reveals better solutions than either of you could have found alone.

Trouble develops when disagreement is accompanied by uncontrolled emotions. These emotions may range from blind anger to bitter sarcasm. They may be marked by such different feelings as resentment, or hostility, or the desire to prove that he is wrong, and I am right, or the wish to exhibit an air of injured innocence. Remember, disagreement is part of marriage and, by itself, does no harm. The damage is done by the eruption of heated

emotion. Handled in a good spirit, however, your differences will deepen and enrich your love. The main
thing is that you learn how to cope with tension and
with the feelings which often accompany it.

SOURCES OF FRICTION

Obviously it will be important for you to become
aware of those issues around which marital problems do
arise. This book has been planned to help you deal with
the most common sources of friction. Also, you may
foresee special problems, not mentioned in this book,
which you ought to bring out into the open as part of
your preparation for marriage.

The list can be staggering and has been known to
scare some people away from marriage altogether. If
the hazards seem great as you look ahead, remember
that marriage is no frivolous matter.

The tragic dramas re-enacted daily in the divorce
courts and the twisted personalities of thousands of
children who were caught up in the tragedies are sober
warning to all of us who expect marriage to be easy. The
vast majority of divorced people looked like you when
they were planning their marriage. They were sincere,
"in love," thoughtful about each other—and positive
that their marriage could not end unsuccessfully.

OPEN LINES OF
COMMUNICATION

Your list of possible marital hazards will lead quite naturally to the next step in their solution. You will want to talk frankly with each other about what you would do in each different situation. What will you do if you notice yourselves becoming angry or bored or chilly with each other? When will you seek outside help by going to a marriage counselor?

Actually you will find that such a conversation, before trouble even appears, will strengthen your marriage later. You will not be caught completely by surprise. Invariably, the people who are off guard are the most vulnerable in a crisis. But you will have been working out tentative solutions to future problems. You may not hold yourselves slavishly to your earlier solutions. You will, however, have learned that answers are available to every problem, and you will have discussed a way to solve it.

Moreover, in discussing problems before you yourselves have become involved in them, you will be free from the emotional overtones which make candid discussion difficult. You will have been learning how to keep your "lines of communication" open to each other so that you can talk easily to each other and view your problems with a degree of detachment. The ability to share opinions on an intellectual rather than an emotional plane can be a needed safeguard as well as a great delight in your marriage.

A happily married friend of mine says that she and her husband struck a bargain before they married to allow no festering feelings to develop between them. Their policy is to keep everything open and straightforward. They have learned fruitfully how to exchange ideas with each other. But they have learned that communication is more than talking. It includes an exchange of feelings, before those feelings get bottled up and eventually explode. "No festering allowed" might be a good slogan for any marriage.

WHEN FEELING RUNS HIGH

Sometimes your feelings run beyond the reach of detached discussion. They seem to rise, often suddenly, out of the deepest parts of yourself. You cannot simply talk about them because you feel them so intensely. On such occasions it may help you to have several things in the back of your mind.

First of all, it is healthy for you to have some safety valves available. The wife who can chase dust or pull weeds viciously out of the garden has a fine outlet. The husband who can go to the basement and begin to hammer nails has a wonderful way of expressing his most aggressive feelings. Often you can walk around the block or find similar ways to redirect your feelings without slashing out at each other.

The spoken word, however, possesses a treacherous quality when used at the peak of strong emotions. People who would not dream of throwing rolling pins or using knives to cut each other do sometimes use words as a substitute. They aim to hurt each other. Words, so used, can be very damaging to the relationships in marriage. A word not spoken is still under the control of silence. But once it leaves the lips, a word begins a strangely independent life of its own. It cannot be brought back or quieted. It can arouse other and deeper emotions. It can be the cause of lasting regret.

Of course, you will want to talk frankly with each other about your feelings, but that should come at another time, not when the feelings are running strong. Self-control in what you say is a good practice, especially when you are feeling upset or likely to hurt each other.

Secondly, you will want to be ready for occasional face-to-face outbursts. At these times, especially, you will need to show understanding in your love for each other. For example, some women find that for a few days before their menstrual period they get increasingly tense or moody or unreasonably irritable. When the period actually begins, though, the nervous pressure ends. The thoughtful husband who understands this fact can help his wife by being more tender and more restrained with her during those few days.

Similarly, many men bring home from their job an accumulation of anxiety and frustration. When a man gets angry with his boss but cannot tell him off, he may bring his anger home and turn it on his wife. The thoughtful wife will try to understand. She can help her husband face a job which he may be keeping largely for the sake of his family's financial security.

Many times our exhibitions of temperament are not caused at all by the hapless person who catches the brunt of them. It is, in fact, a tribute to the security we feel in our homes that we can bring out feelings there which we are unable to express anywhere else. The wise and thoughtful spouse will try to remember that he is not the reason for many of the emotional outbursts he hears. He will try to understand the real cause behind them.

One important practice in marriage is this. Never go to sleep on a note of anger or irritation. Your love runs deeper and is more important than your changing moods. Always take time to express your love to each other before you go to sleep.

In the third place, you may sometimes find yourself confronted by strong feelings which you can neither understand nor control. Agree now that you will seek outside help if this should ever happen to you. Before your disagreement becomes a matter of stubborn pride, or curdles your love, go promptly to someone who has the skill to help you. Usually this person will be a professional marriage counselor or a trusted minister or a doctor. An early visit to a competent professional counselor can save you years of heartache later.

WHERE TO GO FOR HELP

Throughout this book we suggest a number of situations in which you may wish to turn for help to a competent professional counselor. Some of these occasions may arise before you even marry; others may occur twenty years after your wedding day. At such times you may feel a pressing desire to obtain assistance, but you may not know anyone to whom you can go with confidence. How can you avoid the occasional mountebank who claims to be a marriage counselor?

How can you discover the person who will really help you?

Your friends or your family may have suggestions to make. They may know someone who has a good reputation or someone who, they think, *ought to be good* because of the high price he charges for his services.

But you will be on safer ground if you seek the opinion of a person who has had wide experience with the counselors in your vicinity. The student adviser or dean of a college may have had such experience, or you might ask the advice of a trusted minister or doctor. Most cities have family service agencies as a part of their United Fund or Community Chest. The caseworkers in these agencies are well-trained and experienced professional people. Often a caseworker is the best possible resource for those who need marital counseling. Or, if you need more specialized assistance, you can be confident that a family service agency will refer you to the most able specialists in your community.

LOVE, HONOR AND CHERISH

A beautiful prayer, which is frequently included in the Marriage Service, asks God that this couple "may so love, honor and cherish each other that their home may be a haven of true blessing and peace." It is a noble petition, and one word in it reaches the heart of how to handle disagreements in marriage. This word is "honor."

Honor is the necessary ingredient in mature married love. It suggests respect, loyalty and a firm code of behavior. Honor puts backbone and stability into what could be a fleeting emotion. When two people honor and cherish each other, it is possible for them to disagree without altering the depth of their love.

Sometimes at parties I have met a husband and wife who snipe openly at each other. Each seems determined to put the other in his place. Affectionate teasing between them has disappeared. Instead their humor is barbed with sarcasm. Such a display, even if disguised, always depresses me. I have a feeling that here is a marriage with little honor left in it. Sometimes I catch an expression in the husband's eyes as he looks at his wife. "I don't respect you any more," it seems to say. Or I notice that the wife is studying another man, as if to say, "Why did I make such a stupid choice?"

A couple like this may be a long way from the divorce courts and may still be able to recover what they have lost. But, for the moment at least, the joy of being in love seems to have gone out of their marriage. They no longer have a sense of mystery and wonder about each other. One no longer expects to be surprised by the other.

On the other hand, I have known couples married many years who are not contemptuous of each other. Their love has deepened into a mature and wonderful thing because of their mutual respect. Little things they do, small courtesies, show the esteem one has for the other. The husband may buy flowers for his wife occasionally or escort her proudly, as though she were still a bride. And she, in turn, seems delighted every time he comes home from work, or she prepares meals she knows he likes.

A couple like this has disagreements, often many of them. But they have kept that special attitude of honor. They may play and joke and tease. They may argue about many things. But under all the differences runs a mood of deep respect. Each sees the other as a precious person, infinitely mysterious, desirable and lovable. Disagreement holds no threat where honor is still present in a marriage.

Practical Tips

The goal in marriage is not to think alike, but to think together.

WHEN ANGRY OR IRRITATED

Be particularly thoughtful of each other when you are talking about something which touches your feelings deeply.

When you are under pressure, are your reactions calculated to hurt the other person? If so, can they be turned into more creative and harmonious channels?

Make a point, before you go to sleep, of expressing your love to each other. Love needs to be expressed in order to grow.

Develop the practice of saying your evening prayers together at the end of each day. More will be said in Chapter 9 about the use of a family altar.

ABOUT THE HONEYMOON

Remember that tension is often high at the very outset of marriage. You are likely to be unusually tired and strained. So plan your first days together to get relaxed and rested.

Know where you are going after the wedding, and have reservations made. I know several couples who have suffered the humiliation of spending the first night of their wedded life in their car.

Be especially tender and thoughtful of each other in the opening weeks of your marriage. This applies particularly to the sexual relationship. Sex is treated in more detail in Chapter 3. But remember, great gentleness and consideration are important as you make the first adjustments to being married.

A Book About Handling Disagreements

Fromm, Erich. *The Art of Loving*. Harper & Brothers, New York.
A psychiatric approach toward tension, emotional problems, and maturity in human relationships.

CHAPTER SEVEN:

Handling social problems

SOME PROBLEMS can sneak up on you so insidiously that you are completely enmeshed in them before you realize what has happened. If someone had warned you of them in advance, if you had been able to see what was developing, if you had agreed upon a strategy for handling them, you could have avoided endless remorse. The purpose of this chapter is to help you anticipate some of these problem situations. Then you will be able to talk about how you will meet them.

THE MOTHER-IN-LAW
PROBLEM

Some people will be especially close to you and to your family. They will know you well enough to speak frankly to you. They will love you enough to want to help you. Many times they will be your strong right arm, your help in sickness, your encouragement in despondency, your source of fellowship in loneliness.

But these same people can present some of the most deceptive blockades your marriage will meet. Because they have access to your heart, they will be able to twist your feelings and confuse your loyalties. Usually they themselves will not realize how deeply they are disturbing the primary relationship between a husband and a wife. Often they can do their greatest damage while sincerely believing that they are helping you. There are many times in marriage when a husband and wife have to be left alone. At these times anyone who enters your rightful privacy becomes an intruder. And you will find that three groups of people can become intruders in your marriage. They are you own relatives, your friends, and your children. Each group in its own way can pull you apart from each other.

Because we have called this section "the mother-in-law problem," let's look first at your own relatives to see how they can become a disruptive force in your home. Any relative can cause you trouble, and perhaps your mother will be the one. As you have children of your own, you will be vastly more sympathetic toward her, even as you resist the problems she creates. You will see clearly how you yourself may become a difficult mother-in-law.

The vocation of the mother is within the home, in raising children. As her children grow up and marry, she begins to lose a major purpose in life. Often she cannot cope with this change and has no alternate resources to take up her energy and her time. She, then, tries to hang onto her own children and their children, running their home as she used to run her own. She has a powerful hold upon your heart. You owe her respect and loyalty. And, unless she is a very mature and stable person, she may press her advantage over you unconsciously.

Your mother will remember you as a helpless little baby. She will remember the times she had to change your diapers and arbitrate your fights; the times you came crying to her for comfort. She will find it hard to believe you are grown up enough to have your own family. And she will be right—you are not old enough or experienced enough to run a home. No one ever is at the start of a marriage. She herself was not.

But this is the point: you are going to have your own home. You have both the right and the responsibility for its care. Of course, you will make mistakes, but probably no more mistakes than your own parents made. You will need to help your relatives understand that your home is your responsibility and not theirs. When they visit you, they come as your guest. They will be welcome, beloved, respected, but still guests.

So, when your mother comes to visit, she may enter your kitchen as though it were her own. She may shop for you, and rearrange your spice shelf, and tell you what is wrong with your cooking. She may want to alter the furniture in your living room. She may speak freely her disapproval of your theories of child raising. She may express her views of your own relationship, that the husband is not spending enough time at home, or that he is always underfoot instead of going out and being a good provider. She may not like your friends, or your community, or your social habits, or the books and magazines you read. And on all these matters she may be right. Her wisdom may be far greater than your own. This is one reason why her unsolicited advice may trouble you profoundly.

To meet the problem you will want to keep clear

in your minds and hers the difference between un-wanted advice and those points where you have really sought her help. You will find certain things which can give her opportunities to help you. You will al-ways want to be sympathetic, understanding her prob-lems and her needs. But sometimes you will need to be firm, asking her flatly to respect the procedures of your home.

The secret of your success, of course, will rest upon how closely husband and wife stick together. If you show no open disagreement with each other, if you are constantly united when you are in public, if you are insistent in your support of each other, then your mar-riage will be invincible. No one will be able to divide you. Some of the most upsetting problems of marriage begin when a wedge has been effectively driven be-tween you, when you are openly holding different opinions, or when one of you secedes and gives pri-mary loyalty to someone else.

In the privacy of your own bedroom, of course, your real differences will have to be expressed, your real anxieties and tensions will have to come to the surface. You will need to be alone to talk about your changing perspectives and revised ideas. But when anyone else is around, you will want to give the appearance of harmony.

WITH YOUR FRIENDS

The same approach applies equally well with your friends. Sometimes, with the worthiest intentions, a friend will plant doubts in your mind as to the faithfulness of your marriage partner. Or a friend will sow seeds of dissension between you about the use of your leisure time, or about the way to spend your vacation, or about the way to handle your children. Or your friends will press you into so many clubs and social groups that you have no time for each other.

Once again, the soundest procedure is for you to present a united public front. When you have serious doubts or disagreements, they should be aired only when you are alone together. Then you can talk them out, reach your understanding, and emerge from your private conversation looking like an harmonious couple.

The one occasion—and the only one—when you may talk frankly to someone else about each other, will be when you are trying to solve a problem which you cannot solve alone. Then you will want to seek the aid of a competent and professional counselor. In such a person's office you may talk freely, in the conviction that your talk is completely confidential. In some marriages the time does come when such help is needed.

You will find release and comfort in being able to talk honestly about your anxieties. But this talk should be limited to the offices of a professional counselor, a minister or psychologist, a psychiatrist or family case worker.

INTRUDING CHILDREN

Of all the intruders who can wedge themselves between you, your children will be the most pervasive and often the most clever. At an early age children develop an uncanny ability to detect which parent will be firm and which will be soft, which will allow loitering at bedtime, and which will give the candy. They will play the mother for one advantage and the father for another. They will try to play you against each other. They will work to get each of you to show favoritism to one child instead of another.

The real answer to everyone who intrudes—whether they are relatives, friends or children—rests upon your firm intention to back each other wholeheartedly. Many people will try, from time to time, to turn your marriage into a triangle. You can avoid their intrusions by airing your grievances when you are alone with each other, or when you are in the presence of a professional counselor, and at no other time.

ALCOHOL

Alcohol presents one of the most serious social problems our nation faces today. Every minister sees its disastrous effects on human lives and is impressed with the staggering size of the problem. Alcohol is mentioned more frequently in divorce actions than any other single factor. The number of problem drinkers in our country is increasing at an alarming rate.

The fundamental human issues raised by the use of alcoholic beverages seem to be almost as old as mankind itself. An ancient story in the Old Testament speaks of the drunkenness of Noah, the man who survived the Flood and became the "first tiller of the soil." In our own time these basic issues have been made more intense and more complicated by the pace and pressure of our life, by the easy availability of alcoholic drinks (especially such potent beverages as whiskey, gin, rum and vodka), and by the spreading social acceptance of cocktail parties. The rapid national rise in alcoholic consumption makes this a subject which should be carefully considered as you plan your marriage.

Various branches of the Christian church are all agreed that excessive drinking is seriously evil. They all encourage moderation, and many Christian groups flatly favor total abstinence. Though historically its strength is relatively recent, there is, in modern Protestantism, a very strong temperance movement which opposes the use of every kind of alcoholic beverage. But this position is not limited to Protestantism. It has well-informed and ardent advocates in every branch of Christianity. The reasons behind abstinence are weighty. They deserve your thoughtful attention as you make your marriage plans.

Three approaches to the question of alcohol are available to every couple. You will have to choose one of these alternatives yourselves, and you will need to be prepared to face the consequences which may arise from your choice.

In the first place, there is the course of total abstinence. This is, by far, the safest approach. If you agree to abstain completely from all alcoholic beverages, and if you stick to your agreement, the dangers which go with drinking will never upset your marriage. You will not be leading others, by your example, into habits that may be hurtful to them. You will not have anxiety about what your example may do to your children. And you will certainly save money. As a matter of principle you will be agreeing that alcohol will have no place in your marriage.

But total abstinence also poses very real problems

for some couples. In some parts of the country, and in many social groups, the pressure to drink is very great. If "everyone does it"—at least everyone you know—you may feel like a sore thumb when you stand out in the crowd. Sometimes you may meet a hostess, too, who is prepared to offer you nothing but alcoholic drinks. Will you embarrass her and other people if you refuse? How will you handle the astonishment of someone who assumes that everyone will have a drink? For some people the social pressures seem almost too great to resist. So you will want to remember that a firm but pleasant refusal is easier than later battles against an enslaving habit. It is quite possible to say, "No, thank you," and still maintain the respect of other people. In fact they are likely to respect you more because you do have principles to which you adhere.

A second approach is to drink only those beverages in which the alcoholic content is relatively small—a glass of wine or of beer. Many people of French, German, or Italian background, for example, drink wine and beer as casually as they do water. They expect to drink in moderation with their meals. They expect to drink in their own homes or in the homes of friends, rather than at bars.

The danger of this approach is that some people do

become problem drinkers who never touch anything stronger than beer or wine. Skid row has many inhabitants whose consuming desire is a bottle of wine. They need nothing stronger to satisfy their craving for alcohol. While many people can drink these beverages in moderation all their life, there is always a percentage of those who cannot tolerate alcohol in any form. No one can predict who will fall into this percentage, but it can be heartbreaking if it happens in your marriage.

A third approach is to agree to drink all kinds of alcoholic beverages, but in moderation. Moderation, of course, is the goal of everyone who plans to drink at all. No one begins a lifetime pattern of drinking with the intention of becoming a problem drinker. On the surface, this plan to drink in moderation seems like a reasonable approach and one which ought to be easy to maintain. The trouble is that the way people use alcohol is not always as reasonable as they may intend. The problem is complicated by the fact that, as yet, there is no way of predicting who will become a problem drinker.

Some people in their early twenties are already drinking compulsively. If, during your courtship, the drinking patterns of your partner trouble you, then is the time to face the problem frankly. Getting married will not settle the matter for either of you. It is likely to become more intense until, perhaps too late to do any good, you have to admit that alcohol is ruining your marriage. It is far better that you should try to work out a solution before you marry.

Many problem drinkers, however, are not recognizable until they are forty or fifty years old. They will have been showing danger signals long before that age, but it may take that long before they are visibly drinking too much—beginning to miss work, becoming ill, and showing signs that alcohol is more important to them than family or work, marriage or life itself. Many problem drinkers emerge from the large group of moderate drinkers. For years they have seemed able to control their drinking.

If you expect to be moderate social drinkers in your home or with your friends, you will do well to look many years into the future. Plan to stay alert to each other's drinking patterns. Agree now upon some cues by which you may reopen the question as to whether it is wise for you to drink. And, if you agree that alcohol may be raising a many-headed problem for your marriage, then agree to get some help and to stop using it altogether.

YOUR PART IN THE
COMMUNITY

There is a good reason for requiring witnesses at every marriage and for opening the marriage service itself by seeking the approval of these witnesses. The reason is that no marriage stands alone. You cannot keep your marriage from contact with the world around it. Those families which determine to live for themselves alone are effectively planting seeds of marital weakness. Your community needs your contribution to its welfare, and your marriage demands that you participate responsibly in the community.

You will want to plan together ways that you will try to serve your community.

It may be that you are especially interested in something like a church or settlement house or social agency. You may help solicit money for these institutions. Perhaps you can offer a particular talent like painting or craft work, music or hobbies, leadership education or administrative skill.

Perhaps some cause has captured your imagination:
conservation,
or the missionary movement,
a parent teacher association,

mental health,
world peace.
It may be that you would be willing to serve but have
no special concern or skill of which you are aware.

Do plan, now, to take your full part in the life of
your community. You will be surprised at how your
marriage is strengthened by carefully selected outside
interests. Your own horizons will be expanded until
your home will have wide windows open to the world
around it.

Of course, you will want to discover that balance
which every marriage needs, between interests inside
the home and those outside it. You will do well in the
early years of your marriage to find the right mixture
for you. Good marriages make good communities, and
a good community can bring great strength to your
marriage. Plan now your contribution to the world
in which you will live.

Practical Tips

In marriage you belong to each other. Allow no one
—relatives, friends or children—to drive a wedge
which will separate you from each other.

Allow yourselves frequent spaces of time to spend just with each other. This will be most difficult—and perhaps most important—during the years when your children are small.

When you do have disagreements, do not air them in front of other people. Especially when your feelings are sharp, be careful. Sometimes angry words reveal strong feelings; more often, bitter and cutting remarks show them.

You cannot constantly be chopping each other down without chopping at your marriage, too. So, listen carefully to yourselves to see whether a note of frustration or disappointment or hostility is creeping into your talk to each other.

Be ready to use a professional counselor as often as you feel the need.

The safest, surest way to handle alcohol in your marriage is to agree that neither of you will drink at all.

If you are going to use drink in your home, use it with caution, recognizing the danger of alcoholic beverages and looking years ahead to its possible results.

Work out an inconspicuous signal each of you can

use at parties, to caution the other, tactfully, not to drink any more. Then, don't be angry when the signal is used.

Plan to take your civic share in the community where you will live.

CHAPTER EIGHT:

Change—liability or adventure?

A YOUNG woman, having married a fine man, after several years of courtship, set out confidently with her new husband to live in a distant corner of the world. Later she told me that their marriage faced one of its severest tests during their first ocean voyage. The reason was that her husband caught a cold. Normally gentle and thoughtful, he was a different kind of person when he was ill. He became abrupt, gruff and impatient.

He would not let her nurse or care for him. He just wanted her to leave him alone. And she, a romantic new bride, began to wonder what kind of man she had married. Trapped on a ship with this stranger for a husband, she wept herself to sleep and yearned for escape.

The purpose of this chapter is to help you anticipate change in each other, in the conditions of your life, in what you expect of marriage.

How will you adjust if the personality of your spouse changes?

Or if you, yourself, become a different person?

What will you do if you have to face a serious illness together?

Or death?

Will it make a difference in your marriage if you become very rich, or very poor?

If you move to a new part of the country?

If you change your kind of work?

If you enter a new circle of friends?

If your religious beliefs are altered?

Today, it may seem impossible to you that any change could occur in your relationship. But change always accompanies growth. You want to grow in your

marriage. The question to face is how you will meet
the inevitable fact of change.

Often the alterations in marriage take place slowly
and by mutual agreement. When you agree to leave a
city apartment and buy a house in the suburbs, you
are united in your desire to begin a different kind of
life. You are ready, together, to meet the new conditions and social pressures of suburban living. Because
you are agreed in the desire for change, you will be
better able to adjust to your changing way of living.

You may encounter drastic change in your job or
financial status. You may marry when you are a threadbare medical student, or chemist working on his doc-
torate, and then in ten years be faced with breath-taking
increase in income. You may be a white collar worker
for sixteen years, then lose your job in a recession and
have to take anything you can get—perhaps what, to
you, might seem a humiliating job as an outdoor day
laborer. You may whiz up to a top executive job which
pushes you into social responsibilities or a publicity
limelight for which the girl you married is completely
unprepared. You may make a vocational switch into a
taxing job which takes you away from your wife and
children far more than she ever anticipated. Will she
be able to take the loneliness, the pressure, the respon-

sibilities for children and house which the wives of the busiest men have to assume?

Sometimes outside forces, over which you have no control, seem to mould your marriage. You are helpless to alter the course of events, and all that matters is how you adapt to the changes that are pressed upon you. Then your vows are really tested, because when you marry, you agree to take each other "from this day forward, for better for worse, for richer for poorer, in sickness and in health."

Two of the most frequent factors that lead to change are sickness and death. We shall now examine briefly how sickness and death can affect the relationships of marriage. Then we shall review several ways of meeting change. We shall see that it is not necessary to fear the strange and the unexpected. Even when caused by the most unhappy circumstances, change can bring new depths of beauty, gentleness and joy to married love.

SICKNESS AND DEATH

In marriage, a serious illness can affect the personality of the one who is well almost as much as the one who is sick. It can alter the habits two people have formed and the relationship they have developed. It can raise such haunting questions as, "Why has this happened to us?" or "What is the purpose of our living?" Sickness can lead to bitterness and self-pity, or it can increase tenderness and self-forgetfulness. It can cause tension and irritability, or it can deepen the springs of gratitude. Serious illness can start to pull a husband or wife apart, or it can bring new foundations of unity and love to their marriage.

For example, when a man learns from his doctor that he has a bad heart, the new knowledge is bound to affect his wife profoundly. She may nag him about doing too much, or she may use her imagination to develop quiet interests for them both to pursue. She may secretly resent the restriction of late hours and crowded schedules of entertainment, or she may be grateful to God to have her husband still alive. Together they may make plans to remove the pressures of their living so that they can enjoy many more years of married happiness. If they can both recognize the necessity for change and agree upon plans for the future, the doctor's warning can be the beginning of a new kind of life together. It can uncover unsuspected resources of love and gentleness and mutual thoughtfulness.

Serious sickness is always unwelcome and unexpected. It brings heavy financial drains in addition to the burdens of physical pain and mental upset. The strains it places upon a marriage are many: secret recriminations, feelings of guilt, a sense of not being understood. Sometimes it forces a change in the roles we normally assign to a husband or a wife.

When a wife is paralyzed with polio, for example, or put to bed for several years with tuberculosis, the husband often needs to become a housekeeper, cook and mother. He needs to develop special qualities of tenderness and compassion. He needs to encourage his wife and let her know that everything is running smoothly and assure her of how much he needs her. Or, when a husband is crippled because of an automobile or hunting accident, the wife often has to become more manly, handling business problems and making unfamiliar decisions about plumbing and household repairs. At the same time that she nurses him, the wife will want to fan the spark of fight within her husband, giving him courage to lead a man's life in spite of handicap.

While serious illness forces sudden and often dramatic changes in the patterns of marriage, death also brings change, sometimes dramatic but sometimes subtle and perplexing. Death within the marriage itself would appear to dissolve the union, because the vows say explicitly, "till death us do part." But the adjustments are hard to bear and continue long after bereavement. Being widowed and facing life alone is particularly difficult if the marriage has been happy or long. Grief also gets tangled up with legal problems and financial strains and all the choking memories that go with readjustment. Imponderable and insistent questions hover constantly around, unanswerable questions which demand to be answered. Why? What has really happened to the one who dies? Will we ever meet again? Is there any future left for me? And always one question keeps returning. Why?

Even where death does not strike immediately at the husband or the wife, it can still bring emotional havoc to the marriage.

One young man, for example, had three close friends die within one year. Normally gay and carefree, he became morose and depressed during that year, and alarmingly introspective. Of course, the change in him changed his marriage.

Sometimes the death of an overbearing parent, or of a parent who has been sick for years will have its subtle and unsuspected effect.

Sometimes the death of a child will bring a couple abnormal grief and will shake the foundations of a good marriage. Death in any form is always a shock. It leaves us with the emptiness of loss, and it reminds us that we, too, will die. But sometimes death is complicated by other undertones of feeling.

Guilt is one of the most common complications to accompany grief. The feeling that I did not do enough or that I did something wrong, the thought that I should have been the one to die, the belief that I could have been more thoughtful, more careful or more loving— these feelings mixed with grief are often paralyzingly potent. Sometimes, too, death brings a sense of relief. Perhaps it ends a time of hopeless suffering, or finishes a burdensome responsibility, or stops a cause of bickering friction. Then there is often a sense of guilt at feeling relieved!

In any event death and illness work their strange and sometimes hidden changes in human lives. Our concern with them here has been to notice how dramatically they can change a marriage.

MEETING CHANGE

But now we need to ask how a couple at the outset of their marriage can be prepared for such changes as we have been considering. How can anyone, even the most mature person, be ready for such cataclysmic change as death or serious sickness? The answer, of course, is that no one is ever completely ready, as no one is ever fully prepared for marriage. There is danger and risk in all the great opportunities of life. Part of the fun of being married is the joy of facing the adventures of life together. Three attitudes, however, can help you when changes come. Reducing the element of risk they can increase the joy of your common adventure.

First is an attitude of candor between a husband and wife. As long as you can talk honestly and directly with each other about the real problems of your common life, you will have a precious source of marital strength and insight. One of the major themes of this book is that your marriage will flourish as you learn to talk things over. Your own marriage mate is the first and natural person with whom to share your concern about changes taking place within your marriage. If you do no more than to encourage an attitude of listening to each other, you will be strengthening your marriage. Especially when we are worried or disturbed, it matters that someone we can trust be ready to listen to us. There may be times when you will want to talk about some things with your family or friends. Anyone who will listen can be a help. But surely your first, natural impulse, when faced with some puzzling change, will be to talk it over with each other. The comfort of such mutual sharing will come most easily to those who, from the beginning of their marriage, have encouraged a free, honest and loving exchange of opinions.

Second is a readiness to seek skilled professional advice. Sometimes, especially in illness, you cannot talk to each other, because one person is too sick to be worried or too weak to talk. Sometimes you are both overwhelmed and confused by the events which are changing your life together. Neither of you quite understands, or can interpret to the other, the complicated forces of change. Hidden reasons and subconscious desires may be working against your understanding. When you are having to cope with death, for example, you may need a well-trained guide before you can see the tortuous complexity of your own grief, or the invisible pressures which are making you hurt your own marriage. Don't insist on muddling through by yourself. If you go for help to your minister, a good psychiatrist, clinical psychologist or family service agency, you may be clearing the way for a stronger marriage than ever before.

Some people feel a kind of shame and sense of personal failure when they have to turn for help to trained professional counselors. But some of the problems we confront in marriage today are too massive for us to handle by ourselves. They are too intricate for the bumbling attention of unskilled advisors. Tackling some kinds of problems alone, we are destined to almost certain defeat. It is far better and more sane to admit that we are only human and to seek the best assistance we can find.

Third, cultivate a willingness to learn and to cherish the truths of your faith. It is a peculiar fact of our time that those spirits which are clamped most tightly against the invasion of religious truth are usually the same ones which have the least religious knowledge to begin with. In your marriage you cannot afford the arrogance of closed or religiously ignorant minds. The power of the Christian faith to unite you and to reveal the deepest reasons for marriage is so great that we shall consider it in detail in the last chapter. Perhaps it is enough to stress here that a living faith, shared by both of you, can bring your marriage strength which you cannot afford to ignore. If your unity is being threatened by change, the God of your faith can bring you courage to face this change creatively. If your marriage is being afflicted with sickness or suffering, the God of your faith, revealed on the Cross, can guide you through suffering to a deeper love. If your marriage is being undermined by death, the God of your faith can lead you to a triumphant affirmation, even over the powers of death. Long before your marriage faces any crises, you will do well to be learning together the truths of your faith.

WHEN ONE PERSON WANTS
TO CHANGE THE OTHER

One further kind of change still needs to be mentioned. This sneaks disruptively into marriage when one person want to "improve" the other. This attitude can be present, for example, when the bride meets the groom at the front of the church and whispers impatiently to him to stand up straighter.

If you believe that you have found a diamond in the rough, if you suspect that all he needs to become an ideal citizen is to be married to you, if you intend to improve his manners or his ambitions or his social graces —pause. Your program to make him over will probably fail, and it may force the failure of your marriage, too.

To be sure, an habitual drunkard does sometimes become a teetotaler; prickly and bitter personalities have sometimes, under the gentle suasions of love, become sweet and gentle people; social boors have sometimes been turned into social charmers. The theme of Pygmalion, so popular in literature, has frequently been true in life. Often marriage has turned a seemingly hopeless creature into a person of warmth and beauty.

But the transformation grows out of genuine love. No one wants to be loved for what he may become. He needs to be accepted for what he already is. Marriage is meant for two people who already accept and love each other as they are.

Practical Tips

Have you planned for medical and hospital insurance, for protection against illness or accident?

Anticipate ways to keep the wife's mind alert enough, her personality flexible enough that she could pick up a job again if she had to. Even when she is immersed in her role in the home, she needs to be developing personal resources that could see her through an unforeseen change.

If you want to be married before the wife finishes school, talk together about what this implies for her ability to get a job if need arose later.

Learn the sustaining truths of your faith *before* a crisis comes.

If you think you are going to change something about your partner, prepare to be disappointed.

A BOOK ABOUT CRISES IN MARRIAGE

SARTON, MAY. *Faithful Are the Wounds*. Rinehart & Company, Inc., New York.
Contains a portrait of a couple who are still torn between love and lack of communication. They reach a new level of tenderness as the result of meeting a major crisis together.

CHAPTER NINE:

Religion in your home

A VERSE from the Psalms says, "God setteth the solitary in families." This is what has been happening throughout your courtship and why you want to get married.

God has been drawing you toward each other until now you want to be joined together in the ultimate union of marriage. God is present as you talk with each other and dream of your future together.

God will be involved in
    the way you use your money
    in the creation of your children
    in your sexual union
    in the contacts you keep with relatives and friends.

God will be deeply engaged whenever you reach the peaks of married harmony or hit painful snags.

God, who created and sustains you, reaches into every moment you are together.

You may not be aware of his presence. You may not always realize his great involvement in your common life. But God makes your marriage possible, as he can make it holy. If you would plumb the deepest meanings of marriage and gaze with wonder at its cohesive power, you will want to look together into the heart of God himself.

MIXED-RELIGION MARRIAGES

Of course, if you cannot share a common faith, it will be difficult for you to share the vision and the mystery of what God has done for you. The tragedy of mixed-religion marriages is that two people are joined in every external way, but cannot be joined at the pivotal center which is the source of marriage itself. Often without even realizing it you will be deprived, because you will be kept apart—yes, forced apart—every time you yearn to explore the true miracle of your life together.

You may feel that you can have a satisfactory marriage without finding a common faith. You may feel that you do not wish to share the religious heart of marriage with each other. You may know of other religiously mixed marriages which seem adequate to you. Certainly it is possible to maintain such a marriage without ending it in divorce, often without too much friction. But the issues which arise in this kind of marriage —let's say between a Protestant and Catholic, or a Protestant and Jew—are serious enough and complicated enough to demand your special attention. If you are thinking of marrying outside your faith, become familiar with these issues before you take the final step. Several good books are suggested at the end of this chapter. You should read enough about the subject to be prepared to meet the obstacles in your way.

Be sure that marriage is more than a physical relationship, more than sociology or psychology or economics can interpret to you. Marriage is more, even, than your will to stay together and your love for each other. Marriage is a gift from God, a miraculous divine event. In its most profound reaches marriage brings you into mystic communion with God himself. But if you cannot speak the same religious language with each other, you will not be free to explore the reality of marriage in its full beauty and holiness.

RELIGIOUS PRACTICES FOR YOUR HOME

Plan, then, before you marry to join the same church together. Plan to let the church enter and nourish your home. If one of you has to convert to the faith of the other, be fair with yourselves before you begin. See if such a conversion is possible. And vow to become active supporters of the church which you join together. The evidence is overwhelming that families which go to church together do stay together.

There are a number of specific and simple practices which you may take into your marriage to remind yourselves that God is with you and to increase your own spiritual perception and maturity. It is well for you to agree upon them now and to begin them as soon as you begin your life together. Your religious habits should be among the first traditions you establish in your home. It is much easier to begin them at the very outset than to drift into ways that have to be rearranged later. It is much better to start your marriage as a natural expression of your faith than to struggle later with self-consciousness and embarrassment about your religion.

One practical suggestion is that you say grace at each meal. Every time you sit down to eat you have reason to thank God—for your growing love, for gifts of food and health and hope, for the comforts and blessings of your home. You may want to speak out loud as you give thanks and take turns saying the prayer. Some families bow their heads for a silent prayer, each person speaking the prayer that is in his own heart. Some families learn singing graces. The children especially like to join with the family in song.

Another helpful practice is the use of the family altar. In the early days of your marriage, you may wish to kneel together at the side of your bed or at a prayer table. There you will pray together, thanking God for another day that you have been together, lifting up to him any problems you may be facing, asking his guidance and protection for your home. Days that are ended in prayer are often emptied of bitterness, and through the night God's silent work continues to strengthen the ties of love. Later, when there are children, you may want to set aside a special place for family prayers, creating around it an atmosphere of devotion. Each member of the family may have something, from among the things he uses every day, he wants to place upon the altar. These objects, together with a painting or piece of sculpture which kindles the spiritual imagination, can form a center for your family's worship. A cross and candles may be added, and from time to time the whole arrangement may be revised to match the seasons and your own needs. A family altar, used for prayers, Bible reading and hymns, can become a place where the great events in your family life can be most meaningfully celebrated. In the morning or the last thing at night, the family can gather there to praise God for holding them together.

Other practices for you to keep in mind are the regular reading and discussion of religious books, Bible study, and regular attendance at the worship services of your church. You need to keep using the language of faith in your home. It will be the only language which can describe adequately the miracle and the mystery and the richness of your unfolding love. One of the best ways to get used to this language is to use it frequently in your marriage. Talk together about a book you are reading, or study parts of the Bible together. And of course, attend the services of your church. When the children are small, there will be times when it will be impossible for you to go together. Alternate, then, one going one Sunday and one of you the next.

THANKSGIVING

You will want to be wary about allowing your religious life to stop with conventional forms of piety. The form can be a mere monument to what used to be, a hollow shell now emptied of real meaning. What you are seeking for your marriage is far more than the pious relics of an indifferent faith. You will want to stop practicing the forms unless there is a transforming faith behind them. You will want to know in the deep places of your heart that God is making a difference in your marriage. You will want to meet Jesus Christ as the Lord of your life together. Your faith will need to be a throbbing, vibrant force.

And so you will keep looking behind the forms of your religious practice to see more clearly how the God of your faith is affecting your life together. When you give thanks to God you will be doing far more than mechanical repetitions. You will be thanking God for specific blessings he has brought to your home . . .

> for the value of your marriage partner,
> for a friend you love,
> for an evening of fun,
> for the intimacies of sex.

You will thank God
    that your child took his first step
    that you could buy a new rug
    that you came home safely from a trip together
    that you can enjoy life so fully . . .
    that your love is growing beyond your earlier
      dreams.

And, then, you will realize the amazing effect of praying out of gratitude. Your awareness of life will sharpen intensely. You will see more perceptively, and listen with greater wonder, and taste with more delight, and touch with increased reverence. You will be learning in your own experience that God is behind every good thing that brings joy into your marriage. In a spirit of overflowing thanksgiving, you will know that God is drawing you ever closer to the one you love.

FORGIVENESS

In quite a different vein, you will learn out of the day to day stuff of your marriage what forgiveness means. Your faith leaps to new life as you do learn, and your whole marriage will be blessed. Suddenly it strikes your consciousness that for months you have been thoughtless of your married mate in little half-noticed ways. You know that, even so, you have been accepted, with no grudge or bitterness held against you. You burst with gratitude that you could be treated so graciously by one whom you had hurt with little acts of thoughtlessness. You understand in a flash of insight that you could have been the cause of small but carping recriminations, the tiny germs of dissension that pile one on top of the other like coral formations until treacherous reefs are formed. Your ways, you realize with chagrin, could have created an atmosphere of disharmony. But you were accepted as you were, forgiven. You vow in gratitude that it will not happen again. And you will strain, by every act of affection and imagination, to make amends.

Sometimes forgiveness goes much farther in marriage than the simple, aggravating little things like forgetting to screw the cap on the toothpaste or sloppiness in personal hygiene or snoring. Sometimes in marriage forgiveness means big and difficult things—infidelity, consistently selfish and destructive demands, compulsive drinking. These are things which strike at the very roots of married harmony. But there have been marriages in which all of these have been forgiven, and the offender has become a redeemed, transformed person. It has been hard, to be sure. But it has been possible with God.

In marriage we can offer forgiveness and receive it too. And in doing so, we learn something about the nature of God, about ourselves, and about that amazing new creation which takes place when "love suffereth long and is kind . . . beareth all things, believeth all things, hopeth all things, endureth all things." (I Corinthians 13)

LOVE

And so love itself, the most beautiful word in the Christian faith, will gain stronger meanings in your marriage. Out of the daily adjustments and acts of loving imagination which go into your marriage, you will discover the warm, life-giving quality of that love which comes from God and seeks its place within your marriage. Love will come to mean more to you than the popular songs express, more than a tickling feeling of elation in the pit of the stomach, more than a kindling of sexual instincts. By themselves, all of these may be essentially empty, or aimed more at your personal pleasure than at the welfare of your beloved.

You will learn of a love which has backbone and enduring strength. When together you sacrifice something for the sake of a child, when together you stand in prayer over your baby's sick bed, when you lose something you had long dreamed of possessing and still rejoice in something your partner has gained, whenever you give yourself away freely and eagerly in the interest of someone you love, then you will be entering the most astonishing dimensions of Christian love. You will, in part, be sharing the love of One who for your sake entered a human body, who for your sake endured a cruel death, who for your sake demonstrated that love and life are triumphantly linked together. You will know in your own heart that love can enter the soul of another person, and can pick up the weights that lie there, and can save them.

One of the nicest symbols of the entire marriage service is the act of joining hands. It portrays, in simple sign language, the warm truth about Christian love. Probably your courtship began when you first held hands, and it has been a symbol of your being together ever since. But had you ever thought how much the open hand, held out in love can mean? A closed fist suggests the extreme opposite of love—self defensiveness and a readiness to hurt. A hand held back reveals a person who is afraid to give his love away, who wants to protect himself against possible mistreatment. But a hand held out in open love is ready to trust, to suffer, to be hurt, and to give itself away. When two people, in a dramatic service of divine worship, extend open and defenseless hands and clasp them together, they are showing to God and to the world their readiness to learn from each other the mysterious penetration of real love.

Books About Religion in Your Home

Pike, James A. *If You Marry Outside Your Faith*. Harper & Brothers, New York.
The best available summary on this subject. It can help anyone to understand more realistically what the problems are in inter-faith marriages.

Baillie, John. *A Diary of Private Prayer*. Charles Scribner's Sons, New York.
One of the best books of prayer for regular use. Designed to start, and to stimulate a person's life in prayer. Prayers are included for morning and evening of a full month.

Morrison, C. G., and Willett, Herbert L. *The Daily Altar*. Harper & Brothers, New York.
Daily readings and prayers for a whole year.

Wynn, John Charles. *How Christian Parents Face Family Problems*. Westminster Press, Philadelphia.
Realistic, practical, and often humorous discussion of the subject. Well-informed and helpful. Most useful for families with children.

APPENDIX

A Few More Books

Most of these are standard works, and the list is only partial. For people who want to read more extensively in any particular subject, many of the books suggested here will refer the reader to additional sources.

GENERAL

DUVALL, EVELYN M., and HILL, REUBEN. *When You Marry*. Association Press, New York.
An excellent book dealing with all aspects of marriage. A classic in the field. Illustrative cartoons, tests, games, charts, diagrams and questions for discussion. Well-written, full of detail, practical and realistic.

MAGOUN, F. ALEXANDER. *Love and Marriage* (revised edition). Harper & Brothers, New York.
Starting with courtship, it traces through the various features of marriage. Style is easy to read; approach is thoughtful and helpful.

ETIQUETTE AND WEDDING PLANS

Post, Emily. *Etiquette*. Funk & Wagnalls Company, New York.

Fenwick, Millicent. *Vogue's Book of Etiquette*. Simon and Schuster, Inc., New York.
Both these books are standards in the field and cover all phases of social usage. They have large sections about weddings. Suggestions about proper procedure, invitation forms, reception plans, dress, and other areas where couples often need practical help.

Hine, James R., and Belting, Natalie. *Your Wedding Workbook*. McKinley Foundation, University of Illinois, Champaign, Illinois.
A manual containing information similar to the two books above. Also pages for keeping lists of presents, guests, etc. Handy, practical.

FOR HOMEMAKERS

Good Housekeeping's Guide to Successful Homemaking. Harper & Brothers, New York.
This book is revised each year and contains articles, pictures and specific suggestions on a wide range of subjects. Decorating the home, food planning, diet, household repairs, care of clothes. These suggest some of the topics.

COOK BOOKS

Do not minimize the importance of a good cook book. The first three titles listed below are excellent booklets on cooking. They are free and may be obtained by writing the publisher whose name is given with the book.

Metropolitan Cook Book. Metropolitan Life Insurance Company, 1 Madison Avenue, New York 10, New York.

Money Saving Main Dishes, Leaflet 239. U. S. Department of Agriculture, Washington 25, D. C.

Facts About Meat. Home Economics Department, The National Meat Institute, 407 South Dearborn, Chicago 5, Illinois.

The next titles are general cook books, planned especially for small family units. They are recommended by home economists, especially if you are just learning how to cook.

HILL, JANET McKENZIE, and LARKIN, SALLY. *Cooking for Two*. Little, Brown and Company, Boston.

WALLACE, LILY HAXWORTH. *Just for Two Cookbook*. William Morrow and Company, Inc., New York.

FARMER, FANNIE. *New Fannie Farmer Boston Cooking-School Cook Book*. Little, Brown and Company, Boston. A good all-purpose cook book.